Dedication

This book is dedicated to my loving family and all those who seek a victorious walk.

Giving Thanks to
God and Our Savior
Jesus Christ

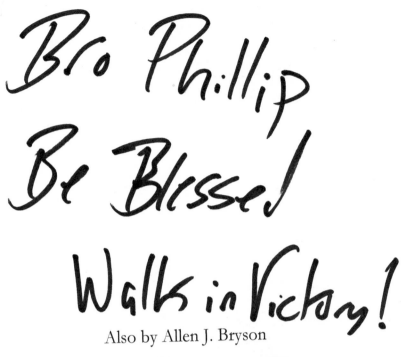

Bro Phillip
Be Blessed

Walks in Victory!

Also by Allen J. Bryson

SMIB

Sleeping With My Eyes Open

Deposit Slips of My Soul

Walk in Victory!

The Ministry of Motivation

Neither Preacher nor Prophet

Allen J. Bryson

EbonyEnergy Publishing, Inc.
Imprint of Highest Good Publications
Chicago, Illinois

The Ministry of Motivation
Copyright © 2008 by Allen J. Bryson
All rights reserved
First Edition 2008

Printed and bound in the United States of America. No part of this book may be reproduced or utilized in any form or by any means, electronic or mechanical, including photocopying, recording, or by any information storage or retrieval system except by a reviewer who may quote brief pages in a review to be printed in a magazine or newspaper, without permission in writing from the publisher. Inquiries may be addressed to the following:

EbonyEnergy Publishing, Inc.
Permissions Department
P.O. Box 43476
Chicago, Illinois 60643-0476

Any resemblance to any person, living or dead unless otherwise noted is purely coincidental. Any errors or omissions in the text or accuracy of the text are accidental. Considerable effort has been made by both the author and the publisher to ascertain accuracy and precision in any objective detail presented.

Library of Congress Cataloguing-in-Publication Data
Allen J. Bryson
The Ministry of Motivation/ by Allen J. Bryson
p. cm.
ISBN10: 1-59825-003-5   ISBN13: 978-1-59825-003-9
1. Title
Library of Congress Control Number: 2008924142

Printed in the United States of America
First Edition, First Printing
Set in Garamond font typeface

Editor: Lynda Bruce
Cover Designer: Barron Steward of Steward Designs

EbonyEnergy Publishing, Inc.
Imprint of Highest Good Publications
P.O. Box 43476
Chicago, Illinois 60643-0476
www.ebonyenergy.com

Acknowledgements

I would like to first thank God and my Savior Jesus Christ for blessing me with the opportunity to reach out to you via my writings. I'm grateful to God for the vision and desire to produce another publication. I thank God for the gifts and blessings of my loving wife Tobi, my trinity of mothers Alice, Marie and Marvine. Thanks go to all my wonderful and supportive (Bryson, Blair, Binion, Wilson, White, Rabb, Jones) family members and dear friends and book club members who have offered prayers, jokes, guidance and encouragement. I offer special thanks to my late father Anderson James Bryson Jr., for making me the man that I am.

I'm thankful for the teachings of Dr. William Winston and my church family at Living Word Christian Center in Forest Park Illinois. Special thanks go to Reverend Greg Blair at Deep Thought Ministries and Mr. Leroy Brown Jr. at Fresh Manna for the Day-Ministries for their contributions of wisdom to this book. I'd also like to give thanks for the encouraging words from the following: Les Brown, Harry Bellefonte Jr., the Reverend Jessie L. Jackson Sr., Sister Vanessa Muhammad, Walter Whitman, Pastor Corey Brooks, The Last Poets, Professors James Anderson and Bill Trent, and Co-Founder of Def Poetry Jam, Bruce George.

A humble thanks goes to every middle school/high school, college/university, church, cultural program, expo, open mic stage and professional organization for allowing me to speak at their respective event. Lastly, I am grateful and thankful to Cheryl Katherine Wash and EbonyEnergy Publishing for their unyielding support and guidance throughout the publishing and marketing process. I am thankful for you all.

Table of Contents

Introduction _____ 13

Route 1: _____ 20

Poetic Pulpit. Verbal Vibes and Verses _____ 20

   Why I write…Again _____ 22

   It Just Ain't…Still _____ 25

   No MTV Rotation _____ 28

   Heart Failure _____ 31

   MLK Today Modern Day Nightmare _____ 34

   The World or the Word? _____ 38

   Grandma's Salute _____ 40

   THEM _____ 43

   What I See _____ 47

   Whom Shall You Serve? Who Are You Serving? __ 48

   Who Am I? I Am Him _____ 50

   What Is That Spirit? _____ 52

   One Less _____ 54

   Hip Hop Holocaust (Triple H) _____ 55

Route 2: _____ 60

Motivational Ministry _____ 60

   FABULOUS FIFTEEN KEYS TO SUCCESS ___ 62

     Key I: Don't Be Afraid To Be Different _____ 66

     Key II: Surround Yourself with Positive People ___ 67

     Key III: Develop Your Mission Statement ____ 69

     Key IV: Keep God in Your Life _____ 72

Key V: Never Compare Yourself to Others _____75

Key VI: Listen to Elders. There is Wealth in Their Wisdom _____77

Key VII: Re-Channel Your Energy/Redirect Your Focus _____78

Key VIII: Sow a Seed_____80

Key IX: Commit Your Life to Knowledge _____84

Key X: Plan "B" Is Not Recommended, It's Required 86

Key XI: Do Not Fear Challenge and Change _____89

Key XII: Watch Your Mouth _____91

Key VIII: "Cool and Cute" Won't Cut It _____95

Key XIV: It's Not About You! _____98

Key XV: Walk in Victory! _____102

From Mind to Movement _____106

Movement I: Don't Be Afraid to Be Different _____106

Movement II: Surround Yourself with Positive People 107

Movement III: Develop Your Mission Statement _____108

Movement IV: Keep God in Your Life _____108

Movement V: Never Compare Yourself to Others_____109

Movement VI: Listen To Elders. There is Wealth in Their Wisdom _____110

Movement VII: Re-Channel Your Energy/Redirect Your Focus _____110

Movement VIII: Sow a Seed _____111

Movement IX: Commit Your Life to Knowledge_____112

Movement X: Plan "B" Is Not Recommended, It's Required_____113

Movement XII: Watch Your Mouth_____114

Movement XIII: "Cool and Cute" Won't Cut It_____115

Movement IVX: It's Not About You! _____ 115

Movement XV: Walk in Victory! _____ 116

THE TREE of CULTURAL TRADITION _____ 117

The Transfer of Cultural and Generational Tradition. _117
The Roots _____ 118
The Trunk _____ 119
Branches and Leaves _____ 120
The Transference of Tradition and Culture _____ 121
What seeds will be planted? _____ 122

Route 3: _____ 125

Stop Listening So You Can Hear Me _____ 125

The Explanation _____ 126
It Just Ain't, Still _____ 126
No MTV Rotation _____ 126
Heart Failure _____ 127
MLK Today Modern Day Nightmare _____ 127
The World or the Word _____ 128
THEM _____ 128
Hip Hop Holocaust (Triple H) _____ 129

Notes _____ 130

References _____ 131

Recommended Reading _____ 131

Tours and Seminars _____ 132

Allen J. Bryson _____ 133

Are You Ready for Victory?

Introduction

Within these pages, I have collected, compressed, and revised all thoughts reflections, venting sessions, prayers and testimonies. My previous reference to them in the last book was deposit slips of my soul. In this attempt, I refer to my duty as seed planting. Within these pages, one will find thoughts neither preached nor practiced, re-written nor rehearsed, confused nor compromised. What you will see is a two fold delivery involving poetry and motivational addresses.

I refer to this as a collage of the following: thoughts, feelings convictions, and passions, reflections of pain, love, awareness, misery, laughter, inspiration, understanding, hope, anger, frustration, praise, redemption, sadness and sanity. You will find biblical references and I admit my delivery may seem somewhat preacher-like. However, I never attempt to claim my words as gospel, or claim to be an all-knowing minister within each circumstance, thus a suitable sub title would be *Neither Preacher nor Prophet.*

However, I feel every person with a story is in some way a poet, songwriter, or storyteller. And though one may not be an ordained minister, we each have a gift that can serve as a ministry to others in need. Our words, testimonies, experiences, perspectives, revelations and warnings can serve as therapy and preventative maintenance to others we share them with. In many ways, that is a ministry because it touches the souls of people.

In particular aspects of the book you will see numerous biblical scriptures. I use these to reinforce my statements from a spiritual standpoint. In addition, my effort is to demonstrate that whatever our situation may be, there is a biblical principle that speaks to every situation.

I chose to take a verbal excursion within these pages by taking the following three routes:

* Route 1: Poetic Pulpit. Verbal Vibes and Verses

In this opening chapter, you will find the continued collection of verbal verses that may sound like short stories or even a call to arms. A continuation of writings from the last book, *Sleeping with My Eyes Open*, this chapter offers more poems that I hope you will find insightful, inspirational, and thought provoking. You will be introduced to verbal visions that reference things such as community responsibility, relationships, abstract anger, childhood memories, spiritual reflection, and other themes. Much reflection, experience and observation fills the fiber of each heartfelt selection.

* Route 2: Motivational Ministry

Are you ready for victory! Are you ready for a better way to live life? Are you ready to lean how the manifestation of positive principles can change your life? This chapter derives from various motivational speeches that I have delivered across the country. Speaking to youth and adults alike, the emphasis is on personifying true personal development that can lead to a healthy and successful way of life. While the ministry of motivation does reference bible scriptures, it is by no means a sermon but more so a service. Numerous bible scriptures are used to support some of the statements presented as well as demonstrating the spiritual influence to much of what you will read.

It is focused on touching the spirit in a way that encourages and inspires any reader to look deeply within themselves, and find truth to their own definition of success and happiness. I

14

introduce the *Fifteen Fabulous Keys of Success*. A list of powerful points was designed to aid the reader in living a fulfilling and successful life. In this section of the book as well as throughout, my hope is to relay something that will motivate, encourage and inspire you to increase your quality of life as well as the life quality of others.

* Route 3: Stop Listening So You Can Hear Me

This final chapter is basically an explanation of chapter one, Poetic Pulpit. I offer explanations and background of the particular poems showcased in the book. Frequently in poetry publications, the reader may not walk away understanding the foundation or original premise behind the poems after they have been read. Within this closing chapter, an attempt is made to demonstrate what were my precise feelings and thoughts as I developed particular selections. It is my hope that you receive clarity from any poem that you may have questioned.

Another reason I am exited about this project is that it is my desire to offer something different to my readers. I wish to offer something healthy, healing, and helpful without falling into the current mode of many authors. The tabloid tapestry is what I refuse to reinvent. It is my hope to present something new, fresh, positive and uplifting to readers. I dare you to read this book and not find something helpful, inspirational or encouraging.

I have witnessed a push in urban literature which glamorizes opportunistic peddlers/thug/gangster/criminal/hyper-sexual/drama filled/*baby's momma*/*gold-digging-hoochie - momma*/cheater/woman beater/who's gay now?-life on the *down low*, chump change chasing/ hip hop, drug dealing, hustling, and pimping.

I am of the belief that READING IS LIKE EATING. Both are activities of substantial consumption. Every day we consume both food and information. The reality is that over a period of time; the things that make us healthy and intelligent (or sick and ignorant) come directly from what we take into our mouths and what we take into our minds.

Additionally, this affects the heart. Just as much of what we eat can destroy us, the same goes for much of what we read. If we fill our bodies with too much fattening, high calorie, chemically enriched, unnatural foods, over a period of time that will affect our physical hearts making us susceptible to cardiac arrest-*heart failure.*

The same thing happens with our minds. If we continue to fill our minds with toxic imagery, statements, beliefs and customs in the long run we can affect what fills our hearts. We then become susceptible to intellectual, spiritual and cultural decay. For what comes from the heart is spoken through the mouth in which our speech plays a major role in our circumstances.

Many have asked, why did I write this book? My motive is quite simple. It is evident that there is a modern day unveiling of an American Pathology that includes the following:

Envy, greed, arrogance, lack of originality, spirituality and creativity, poor decision making, instant gratification, lack of an essential parental obligation, mis-education, child abuse and neglect, meaningless consumption and competition, impressionable duplicating mindsets, deteriorating work ethic, glorification of prison life, crime infested communities, reckless lifestyles, acceptance of death, sickness, fear and poverty, generational distance, juxtaposed with an inability to decipher fantasy from reality.

I wrote _The Ministry of Motivation_ in attempt to attack and aid in the eradication of all the above. It is time for us to live fulfilling reflective yet rewarding lives. It is time to take our exodus from emptiness, unhappiness, despair and an unfulfilled existence.

In these chapters, the phrase WALK IN VICTORY is introduced. This is a slogan that was introduced to me by a dear friend and colleague Dr. Timothy K. Eatman. To _Walk in Victory_ means to develop and maintain a "victorious attitude" about life because of the promise that God has made to us which gives us victory in life over all things.

This is not just a slogan, but a way of life. I say this because at times we are quick to accept and quote scriptures and/or hip and catchy slogans, then go right back to living the same defeated lives, the exact opposite of what we claimed earlier.

In certain arenas of life, we get defeated mentally and spiritually, and we need to be reminded that we do not fight our battles alone for we have a great supporting cast which is love of our families and the power of God. We all need to be reminded of this when times get hard. So I try not to just say Walk in Victory, but to actually believe it and manifest it into my life. And I hope you will be compelled to do the same.

Verbal Vibes and Verses

Route 1:
Poetic Pulpit. Verbal Vibes and Verses

I DREAM OF A VICTORIOUS LIFE!

Why I write...Again

I'm writing again and again and again and again in hopes of redemption and forgiveness of my sins
I'm writing to escape pain from my neurotic membranes and foolish fears
Good thing writing is not a crime, because I'd be sentenced to at least 20 years

You see— even though my life has me wilding and the flow has me styling, cops hidden cameras have me profiling.
The spirit of Marvin is asking me *What's Going On,*
trying to answer difficult questions with visions that I'm flowing on
I live in the city of wind, the city of sin, a city held up by political safety pins

The city of broken dreams, creased jeans, gangster leans, and
at times questionable sports teams
The city where men worship the woman with a higher rear,
and a Mayor named Daley who moves waste like diarrhea

Jill Scott once said that one nightmare shouldn't be the
reason you stop dreaming
Magnificent milestones yet to be reached got me so excited
my momma's screaming
Catch me embracing the heat rays of the sun though this
world is so shady;
Giving power to words that will lift you off the floor like
Kobe and McGrady

I write to release myself from destitution and danger;
so in the midst of the storm I'd dance with a total stranger
While heartache makes some bitter, it makes me better,
so I'm walking out on pain and here's my Dear Jane letter

This is for the cats on the Southside of Chicago
for the cats in East St. Louis forced to lay low
for the cats I've seen in South East DC,
and those pushing hard in the five boroughs of NYC
for the cats in South Central and Watts projects,
and those in the trap of the 5th ward down in Houston, TX

Sick of thugs bragging about what they do in the streets
Sick of babes babbling about what they do in the sheets
I try to separate myself from they way the he goes and she
grows, so I associate myself with a league of uppity Negroes
Jay Z once claimed he'll dumb down for you cats just to make
more dollars,
But if I suggest brothers "Smarten up" for a change,
now they want to scream and holler

Some guys were never taught so how can they teach?
You see them in pursuit of things that are way out of reach

Young 'fools' run around with faces of white gangsters on
their chest like that's so chill
Don't you know, Gotti and Capone would have murdered
you as if your name was Emmit Till?
Guess you don't know who he is either, ask you parents what
this is all about?
The last young man I mentioned Emmit Till to, asked me
"Did he do a video?" And "when is his CD coming out?"

I write because some are driven by the 3 B's;
Babes, Blunts, and don't forget the *Bling*
Will have our babies do just about anything
There's no ice in the fridge because its sits around their necks
Ignorant imbeciles make an oath to steal kill and destroy just
to earn respect.

Feeling *Froggy* so they're quick to jump put a gun in their hand
But you can't pay them to think about doing that over in Iraq
or Afghanistan
I keep a quick step to flee the racist vipers marching to harm
me
I'm so vexed and perplexed for these street soldiers don't
realize they've enlisted in absolutely the wrong army

I've got to laugh to keep from crying
I've got to live to keep from dying
I've got to stay cool to keep from frying
I try my best to be honest because it's so easy lying

Frustrations kicking in make me want to chop this verse
apart, "Shorties" would rather believe in the Tooth Fairy

putting change under their pillows, than Jesus putting change in their hearts

I write because we still live in the land of the hood sons
Clueless sisters sleeping with bad boys not realizing they are sleeping on the good ones
Once they get burned, bruised, baby loaded and labeled as bust downs
They find themselves over 30 and single with three kids crying about *"there are no good men around"*

I try to tell them but they don't want to listen
I try to help them, but they'd rather glisten
Even try to catch them but they choose to keep missing
this message written for the ones who missed a few classes
They are too busy focused on spinning twenty-two inch rims pimp brims, knee high *Tims,* and listening to the masses

This is the mentality that you and I have to battle;
our community has been stuck on *bling* since the days of pacifiers and rattles. They don't want to grow; they want to shine

They don't want to invest; they want to IMPRESS yours and mine. They don't want to create our justice; they want to make others jealous. And for this I'm still writing

It Just Ain't…Still

It just *ain't* man, it just ain't; still, it just *ain't* man,
Every brother-man *ain't* brown

Everyone that's sad *ain't* wearing a frown
Everyone claiming they're hip, *ain't* down
Every shut-eye *ain't* sleep; every grave *ain't* 6 feet deep
Every brother moving in the night, *ain't* trying to creep

Everything sold *ain't* for sale,
Everyone blind *ain't* reading in Braille
Every cat in prison *ain't* in jail
Every doctor *ain't* healing the sick,
Every magician *ain't* showing his trick
Every president *ain't* democratically picked

Every minister *ain't* preaching,
Every classroom *ain't* teaching
Every extended arm *ain't* reaching

Everyone coming *ain't* staying,
Everyone suited up for the game *ain't* playing
Everyone on their knees *ain't* praying, it just *ain't*, it just *ain't*

Everyone wounded *ain't* bleeding,
Everyone asking for help *ain't* needing
Every brother with a book in his hand *ain't* reading

Everyone working *ain't* grinding,
Everyone *Blinged* out *ain't* shining
and some looking for love *ain't* necessarily finding

Everyone claiming victory *ain't* winning,
Everyone asking for forgiveness *ain't* sinning
Your enemy may be ready to attack with anger
yet still in your face grinning
Every tired soul *ain't* weary, every sad eye *ain't* teary
and just because you know the formula, doesn't mean you
understand the theory

Everyone singing lyrics doesn't know the song, just because
you feel bad doesn't mean you did wrong, and just because
you fit in, doesn't mean that's where you belong

Everyone rhyming *ain't* flowing, just because you get bigger
doesn't mean you're growing, and everybody hollering about
heaven *ain't* going

Everyone flirting with you *ain't* winking,
Everyone drunk *ain't* necessarily been drinking
and just because you used your head doesn't mean you were
thinking

Every joke you tell *ain't* funny,
Every bright day *ain't* necessarily sunny
Every robbery and theft *ain't* about the money
Every family *ain't* related, every church *ain't* congregated,
Every thug *ain't* gang related thus, every crime *ain't*
investigated

Every cloud *ain't* bringing rain,
Every cat found guilty *ain't* the one to blame
Everyone shouting "ouch" *ain't* necessarily in pain, dig it?

Every house *ain't* necessarily a home,
Every king *ain't* ruling from the throne
And just because you didn't see it, doesn't mean it *ain't* been
shown
It just *ain't* man, it just *ain't*
It just *ain't* man, it just *ain't*

****

No MTV Rotation

Malicious Terminated Vision/ Black Eroded Thinking
Malicious Terminated Vision/ Black Eroded Thinking

Show me a criminal locked up jail, I'll show you a brother
with property to sell
Show me a thug out hustling and slinging rocks
I'll show you a brother with his eyes on Wall Street Stocks

Show me a young fool clowning and failing in school
I'll show you a genius learning so much that
he's calling the teachers the fool

Show me a posturing pimp riding and hustling tricks,
I show you a doctor at the county hospital healing the sick
Show me a deadbeat dad dodging his kids and child support
I'll show you a coach molding and developing kids just for
the sport

Incredible rays of hope that dwell throughout the nation
It's too bad because unlike losers, brothers don't get that
MTV rotation

Show me a girl prostituting or stripping for loose cash
I'll show you three sisters teaching biology, physics and
chemistry class, working day and night so your kids will pass

Show me a girl lying up with babies drinking a 40-ounce
I'll show a sister managing million dollar corporate accounts
Show me a girl lazy and crazy depending on her looks
I'll show you a sister novelist writing award winning books
Show me an overdose victim headed for the grave
I'll show a motherly minister trying to get your soul saved

THERE ARE passionate powerful queens fighting daily for
vindication,
But unlike these individuals, our queens don't get that MTV
rotation

See our media is too busy focusing on the cat with the hat tilt
Instead of the one teaching–demonstrating–showing us how
that's built
MTV Rotation needs to be shut down like black owned night
clubs with no liquor license
Sadly enough the BET Rotation is even worse
Duplicating–devastation and destruction leading our babies
straight to the hearse
as long as it got a booming system and sitting on 20 inch rims
our seeds are quick to jump up and shout
"aw baby count me in."

Because if *"I got to die, I gotta stay fly"*
To focused on twenty inch rims knee high
"Tims" and trying to be like Ms. Jones and them. Someone
needs to tell these silently slumbering slothful seeds to

Drop the pistol and pick up a pen
Drop the microphone and pick up a microscope
Drop the Ball and pick up a book
Red stop signs may be right in your face
and you'll be to illiterate to understand when you look

Get off the bullets and get in the ballot
Get off the booze and brew and get in the Bible
Get off the corner and corner the market
Quit running from the law and go to law school
Sisters get off the pole and get in the process of releasing
your mind from all this mess which is the very thing you
blame for your stress

29

Turn off the TV and turn on some Stevie and wonder...with
some inner-visions that can take you to a higher ground
Quit starting the fights and start the trends,
for on your thoughts and decisions some young soul may
depend
True royalty seeks higher knowledge to obtain and store it
We can't convince our kids to do a thing if there's no
VIDEO for it
We can't convince priceless daughters to be anything but
divas and dimes, years pass and like clocks with no hands
they still can't tell the time. Our souls have toiled through
spheres of time; our cries are heard through the hills
Now all we're known for on TV is iced out grills, *Laffy Taffy*,
Booties-Basketball, and short lived record deals

Skip *The Real World*; show my babies how to get
The Real Wealth
I don't need you to *Pimp My Ride*,
how about you *Promote My Revelation*
And give me *106 Parks* so my kids can really see what FREE
really looks like

See what MTV rotation fails to tell you is this
Here were are in the post Y2K
More than one decade beyond the 90's, baffled because
Babies born in the 80's
Fail to realize how integration efforts of the 70's
took away the fight and hunger we once had in the 60's
So the result is that now our kids listen to songs by 50
(cent)
while drinking 40's
Fearing the responsibility of their 30's
While riding on chromed out 20's acting like teens

We need to groom ourselves for greatness with no doubt,
fear or hesitation, so in due season we won't need a reason
for the MTV rotation

Heart Failure

Its official, the leading cause of death for black men is, Heart
Failure. Is it HIV, cancer, or violence many of us wonder? I
tell you today it's a failure of the heart that's putting us six
feet under. Sick in the head, sick in the body, sick in mind,
but the sickness of our hearts is what keeps us deaf, dumb,
and blind…anticipating death to sneak up from behind

Suffering from sick bodies where diabetes and hypertension
need our utmost attention for those ailments are placing us
brothers in a physical detention. We brag and boast over
phallic erections and political connections; but after further
inspection, we learn that we have a mental, spiritual, and
internal infection

There's a lack of a decent diet because everything we eat we
have to fry it; now don't even try it saying, "Hey that's how
most black folks eat." That's our culturally clueless way to
deny it

Eating everything with no shame and no exercise and has
been proven to be the express lane to our untimely demise.
You might as well call us life-thieving crooks, because instead
of health and well-being we care more about jobs, cars, and
pocketbooks

Heart failure comes in the face of the heartless—betrayed and afraid— watch as they easily persuade black men to remain silent. The flood of blood meant for our veins cut short and blocked by hunger pains, denying us the power to rise and battle is what this piece implies

Heart failure, our hearts have failed to raise young black babies in the direction of the holy one, watching our children existing empty as we feed their poverty instead of teaching them how to destroy it

Heart failure is where our precious little girls don't know who they are, so now they are titillating targets of the hottest R&B and Rap Stars. Little boys unaware of their own ruthless rages, now makes them the newest animals on display in Cook County Cages, all because of daddy's heart failure

And who in the world told us that it's much better to be a baby's daddy than to be a husband? Like Roy Ayers, freed slaves, and Olympic sprinters, we are "Running-Away" from the Altar because we fear it will in some way alter us; "There's too much pain on that commitment train, yes driver, just give me a ticket for that *Baby Daddy Bus*."

Heart failure is when our hearts have failed to acknowledge the hills from which cometh our help, failure to praise worship and give thanks to the holy one who abundantly blesses is what the minister professes

Watch us as we do drive-by's on churches, which is what we do, we actually drive by churches. Although not so violent, the devastation left behind is never-ever silent as we open fire on congregations with our absence and empty images. The aftermath of our shooting spree shows hundreds of praying women and children drenched in the image of a husbandless and fatherless existence.

Heart failure displays our cranial arteries clogged with insurmountable ignorance. We are always loud and proud about a monetary or physical deed, but silent as thoughts of the night when asked to read.

Watch us give clothes, cash, and toys as each Christmas passes, then wonder why our babies are held back and placed in remedial and special-ed classes.
Never mind blaming the mayor, governor or even the schools, because according to test scores it's the parents who are the fools.
We'd rather drink smoke and party our lives away. It's our way to flee because all that reading brings about too much responsibility, accountability. Oh, get off my back; can't I just be me? We are voluntarily voiceless, seduced into an oblivion of ignorance, living deaf, dumb, and blind.

Newsflash! Living in the 312, 847, 708 or 773, starting from year 2003, watching MJ-23 and B-E-T on that fabulous flat screen TV because of your GED, JD MD or Ph.D, that led to a nice J-O-B, enabling you to drive that luxury SUV down route 83 blasting V103 while carrying a membership card with the NAACP will not make you F-R-E-E!

Brothers please open your 3rd E-Y-E and S-E-E that this is all part of a possible C-O-N-*spiracy!*
Our women are crying and our children are dying because of Heart failure
Our culture is wading and our future is fading because of heart failure
BLACK MEN WE ARE DYING because due to
Flat line_____

33

****

MLK Today Modern Day Nightmare

I have a dream of a 3-day weekend where Negroes will do nothing constructive to commemorate my efforts. They will see my birthday as just another day off work; an extended 3-day weekend where they can party, fuss, fight, freak and floss all in the name of Freedom even though they're just as enslaved now as they were over 300 years ago

They'll have party themes such as MLK freedom bash and ladies night parts 1-2-3 at nightclubs all over the world and not take one second to say thank you Lord for Dr. King and the life he sacrificed for us. This Prince of Peace will be sold for a piece of a price for promotional profits from passed out party fliers. Jesus-Master! I now realize how you feel every 4th week in December

They'll use my name as an excuse to profusely blame white folks for their own discretions, laziness and unwillingness to live up to their God given potential while destroying their minds with weed, Hennessy, and drama. They'll use my name Lord as an excuse to break laws of this land and expect to get off *Scot-free* simply because the arresting officer is white

I have a dream that one day
My four little nieces will be able to take a day off school only to go to the mall and buy stuff they don't need, with money they don't have, to impress folks they don't like,
and flirt with men that they don't know, to indulge in street games they don't understand. New books and computers will be passed up for knee high Timberlands and Coach purses

My four little nephews will continue to replace reading, writing, and education with rapping, dribbling and dunking. Their heroes won't be those who were shot and killed like me, but those who survived shootings and lived to tell about it on a thing called a CD. We will see them jamming and jiving until the break of dawn, their first and only reference to King James will be a teenage athlete named LeBron

They will pay more attention to wheels that spin, than ways to win this battle for freedom through thick and thin. Never learning how to respect and love themselves so they won't learn to do the same with their women. Continuing a cycle of disrespect and abuse of womanhood and the institution of marriage by creating a generation of what are called baby's mommas and baby's daddies. I have a dream today!

I have a dream that one day
Down in ghettos with its crime, cracked concrete, crooked cops, and cooked crack stones where sometimes the light of joy and hope is blown. Loose, lustful, and lost of the lowly will use my birthday as another day to kill each other with the impressionable imported poisons sold to suicidal volunteers whose 3rd eyes has been blinded by the light of addition and instant gratification

They will use my birthday as just another day to steal, kill, and destroy each other through the hatred they see in their own eyes. They will use my day and my name as an excuse to recreate slums they so desperately claim they want to flee. I have a dream today

I have a dream that one day the largest Black television network (for just one day) will show gratuitous 5-second clips of me and say the dream lives on while poisoning the minds of young children by showcasing 24-hours of music videos and promote money flows and clothes. They will say the dream lives on for 2 more seconds before showering you with another 8 hours of booty popping, big *pimpin'*, drug selling, rapper beef battles, ignorant sex songs like *My Cookie, My Milkshake, Pop Lock* & *Drop It* and shake that *Laffy Taffy*

Lord have mercy, I'm not even physically alive, yet my soul can't take this anymore. While babysitting our kids, the popular cable station whose name is an acronym for **B**lack **E**roding **T**hinking, shall teach them to ignorantly sing prophesizing praises of poverty with lyrics like, "Can't pay my rent because all my money's spent, but that's okay because I'm still fly." They will do this in MY NAME Lord!

I have a dream that one day my people will simply get up, rise up, speak up, grow up, pray up, shut up, listen up, lift up, walk up, show up, reach up, look up, stand up, and most of all wake up! I pray they'll see that this dream has become a nightmare that shall hellishly haunt the silent slumber of our children. May the day come where no one will be able to cry *Free at Last, Free at Last, look God almighty, the people are still asleep!*

The World or the Word?

37

****

The World or the Word?

The world is whispering in your ear, but the word is tugging at your heart.
The world is enticing your eyes, but the word is soothing your soul.

The world is feeding your 5 senses, but the word is strengthening your common sense.

The world is telling you to use your brain, but the word is telling you to use your faith.

Listening to the world and NOT the word can make you:

Sabotage your success
Jail your joy
(for the sake of pleasing them)
Postpone your progress
Cripple your condition
(for the sake of pride)
Throw away your thriving
Belittle your blessing
(for the sake of your image)
Destroy your destiny

Hinder your harvest
Abolish your abundance
(for the sake of being rich)
Crush your creativity or

Handcuff your hope
Starve your situation

Imprison your inspiration
Wreck your refuge

Assassinate your aspiration
Frustrate your future

Undermine your understanding
Prevent your protection
Weaken your worth

Pressure your promotion

A powerful minister once asked me: "What are you, a thermostat or a thermometer?" You are a thermometer if you stay where you are. You are a thermostat if you look to where you want to be. Understand a thermometer is satisfied in staying where it is. It does not look beyond the present state of affairs.

A thermostat, on the other hand, looks beyond where it is and it continues to move up to a predetermined setting. In short, a thermometer only moves according to outside conditions. Its reading is controlled by outside forces. On the contrary, the thermostat can control the external forces.

We are now entrenched in the *Reality of Redemption*
So I implore you to never—
Drop your dreams or strengthen the strain of your struggle
Fracture your foundation, limit your livelihood
(for the sake of being cool)
Stifle your strength; hamper your health and healing.
Block your belief or prevent your prosperity
(for the sake of being pretty)

Defeat your dominion or castigate your calling;
Fracture your focus, weaken your worship
(for the sake of popularity)
Slaughter your slumber, derail your deliverance.
Poison your passion or violate your victory
(for the sake of getting a man)
Taint your testimony and fizzle your faith
The world shouts because it's hurting
The word makes you shout because of your healing
The world never lets you forget your sins,
But the word never lets you forget your Savior
The world cries there's a price to pay,
But the word reminds us—HE alone paid the price

The world is saying we need justice;
but the word is saying we need Jesus
The World OR the Word; which are you listening to?

****

Grandma's Salute

Grandmother, Grandma, *Gran-Gran*, Big Momma, or *Nanna*
B. Whether she's known for bible toting or *Virginia Slims*
smoking, she's an elder like no other, we're not here to refute
One in a million, once again it's you Grandma that we salute
A grown folk's party is what she'll create, with Al Green in
the background while you fix yourself a plate

You can catch her in the cut working her master plan.
Eyes aged whether it's her pearls or a glass of gin in her hand
An old school soul music or gospel master so she'll never
miss a beat. Whether it's with her eyes, words or scriptures
she'll cut you deep. So don't cross Grandma, in other words
don't sleep

A strong sister never taking mess from no mister, not even
her baby boy. After giving out whippings to grandkids who
been slipping, She'll fix supper and start singing "you bring
me joy"

While being the oldest of all her siblings,
She surely can tell you what joy it brings to be looked up to.
And the way she plays a hand of Bid Whist, you'd think she
was corrupt to

Because she smiles and glides smooth like two Billie Holidays,
reminding you of those Savoy Aragon Ballroom cat daddy

hustler days. And how she cares for eleven grandkids from
what heaven did, still has us all amazed

And though you can't exactly call her a pastor or a preacher,
Her lessons still ring true, for she is the family's first real
teacher

Teaching the family such lessons such as
Every shut eye *ain't* sleep; every grave *ain't* six feet deep
Everything sold *ain't* for sale;
Every open book *ain't* got a story to tell
Everyone who jokes *ain't* playing,
and everyone you see on their knees *ain't* praying

Everyone seeking the answer *ain't* finding,
Every heavy cloud *ain't* carrying a silver lining
and everyone who's cheating *ain't* exactly two-timing

A character of contagious courage you would think she has a
clone.
Unspeakable how she took 11 grandchildren
and gave them all a home.
Not boasting nor bragging about her deeds unlike most cats.
From chauffer, to counselor, to cheerleader football and big
momma, you see she wears many hats.

From sun up to sun down facing daily duties without *shakin'*
Got so many jobs the neighbors call her Jamaican
Grandma's hands soothed and healed cuts, scars, and sores,
long before prescription medicine was sold in drug stores

Grandma's hands will give you PEACE—
a piece of candy, a piece of advice, a peace of mind
Then she'll turn around and give you a piece of that belt or
switch when you get out of line

Grandma's hands are no stranger to struggle, her efforts
digging deep like a tree's roots
Grandma's hands shared the tears of Billie Holiday when she
sang about Strange Fruit

Grandma's hands are Powerful
*patient-protective-persuasive-proficient-profound-
proactive-profusely-pondering-while-passionately-
paving-pathways-to-predictable-peaceful-paradise-and-
producing-perspectives with prime posture for precious
prosperity while popping pancakes, peppermints, pies
and peach cobbler paired with promising plentiful
prayers.* In short, Grandma's hands are prophetically
perfect.

She makes even the roughest days not seem so hard
and you just look at her in awe, knowing she's touched by
God.
Why some may ask why should we care?
From rising of the moon to the setting of the sun,
she was there—she was there.

Before Max Julian had portrayed the Mack
Before Wendy's came out with the double stack
Before Barry Gordy put Diana on a Motown track
She was there—she was there.

Before Aretha Franklin sang young Gifted & Black
Before Flo-Jo even stepped foot on the track
Before they told black riders to go sit in the back
She was there—she was there.

Before Donny Hathaway & Roberta Flack
Before they put whitewalls on the Cadillac
Before Florida knew James wasn't coming back

She was there—she was there.
So on this day, we celebrate the woman
who takes a little and makes so much for so many
Without the love strength and wisdom of Grandma
some of would us simply wouldn't have any.

****

THEM

He writes because she was wrong, she writes because he left
Now was it left to right or right to wrong?
They both remain writing citing and singing that same old
song
Looking for love in all the wrong places
They are too focused on the beauty, the booty and dollar bills
with big faces
Step right up folks it's the battle of the sexes, battle of the
flexes, from Toledo to Texas
Who's the flavor of the month and who are the soon to be
ex's? THEM

The Spinners once sang,
"It takes a fool to learn that love don't love nobody,
It takes a fool to learn that love don't love no one."
The story goes like this; he's tired of her always being sick;
While she's sick of him always being tired
Now they're both sick and tired of being sick and tired and if
they were working the assembly line of love, they both would
wind up fired! THEM

They both say they want love or do they? Lost in the trap of
external influence and outside definition and need I mention;
they can't be real with each other until they are real with
themselves. Because while she's trying to get to the alter;

He's trying not to get altered

Each of them threatened by competitors from the same
gender; rolling her eyes because that other babe is jiggling a
lot more behind
He's salty because that other brother is flexing too much
shine
Put them together and label them both deaf, dumb, and blind
THEM

He says he'd love to marry her, but he can't because right
now he's engaged to these streets
Full of night time games with numerous victims who lay in
between the sheets
He tells her he can't weather the days nor walk in that maze
of her sanctified lifestyle and celibate ways

Because for every girl that won't stay,
there are ten more that will
For every girl who won't pay, there's four more willing to
foot the bill then move in for the kill
Too many videos with voluptuous angel faced models that
perform ménages like messages
Too many song lyrics telling him show the cars and cash
and he gets easy access to her sacred stash

His boys are chronologically grown men with arrested
maturity levels that play the game of porcupine
(stick and move)
They are so good at what they do; they have formed a secret
society called the Club's R-Us Kids. Their theme song goes;

*"I don't want to grow up, I'm a Clubs R Us Kid, they've
got so many babes up in the club that I can play with,
from 'broads' to lames, look at all of these dames; just sit*

back and watch us run game. Gee Whiz! I don't want to grow up cause baby if I did, I couldn't be a Clubs R Us Kid."

She says she'd love to marry him, but she just pledged a sorority; Delta-Sigma-Drama-Mama. She consumes too many Mary J. Blige songs, Terri McMillan books, and Tyler Perry plays that have hand delivered her a false sense of normality She's constantly believing that he has to be cheating and deceiving which has wrecked her trust. So when a real love comes her way void of the fist-fights, drunken-drama, and two to three baby's mommas, she sees him as boring It's no secret she loves the thugs and the hood sons Constantly sleeping with bad boys not realizing she's sleeping ON the good ones

She feeds on liquor-laced lies and single momma's sweet potato pies that he's too good to be true, for her true love is unattainable Explaining why she has scared off all the men who were once available You catch her in church Sunday after Sunday asking Jesus to bring her the very man that she has already turned away

See she's also a member of the BBS - The Bitter Broad Society consisting of 8 to 10 no-man having friends, aunt's, cousins, and co-workers who haven't had a man since Harold Washington died; filling her plate with *Misery Loves Company*, broiled, baked and fried They call themselves the BBS, but all they're popping is that B-S!

Clueless brothers and unrealistic sisters are holding out like NFL contract negotiations waiting for Mr. and Mrs. "perfect" when they are the farthest thing from perfection themselves

45

They don't understand that they both need to BE that which they seek. Are you what you ask for? THEM

Don't ask for a Halle Berry guys if you look like Biggie
Ladies don't ask for Denzel and you look like Miss Piggy
Don't ask for a drama free woman, but when drama comes you run to get it
Don't complain that he can't buy a thing when you too, Boo, got jacked up credit
Don't ask for Mr. *Down to Earth* when you're Miss *Head Above the Clouds*
Don't ask for a quiet woman when you can't keep from talking loud
Claiming you're not jealous, but when she goes out you hawk her down
You say you're secure but after the break up,
you become the mayor of "Stalkers town"

Guys:
She'll say your money doesn't matter up until the day she gets it
And ladies:
He'll go to church with you every single Sunday, up until the day he hits it

The sad reality is they don't understand that long before the beginning of time they were meant to be, they were one. God ordained it from the rising of the moon to the setting of the sun, they were one

Before the Panthers revolution had turned to black
Before Ike gave Tina a smack
Before inner-city hoods were introduced to crack,
They were one.
Before cigarettes rose to five dollars a pack

Before they told Rosa Parks to go sit in the back
Before Whitney cried out that crack was whack
and before The Terminator said "I'll be back," they were one.

They were meant to be together happy-blissfully, if they only
took the time to set themselves free. THEM
They were meant to be together happy-blissfully,
if they only took the time to set themselves free- THEM

****

What I See

I see love in the midst of hatred; feeding in the midst of
hunger, because of him this is what I see
Learning in the midst of mis-education; wealth in the midst
of poverty

Love in the midst of hatred, feeding in the midst of famine
I see peace in the midst of war, sunshine in the midst of the
storm

Because of him this is what I see. I see the one who loves the
good in me no matter how bad I am

Health in the midst of sickness, smiles in the midst of tears
Growth in the midst of decay, light in the midst of darkness
Faith in the midst of disbelief, pleasure in the midst of pain
Refuge in the midst of danger, strength in the midst of
weakness, triumph in the midst of trials, wisdom in the midst
of ignorance

Because of him this is what I see
I see the one who ensures that no weapon formed against me
shall prosper

I see assurance in the midst of uncertainty, joy in the midst of sorrow, calm in the midst of chaos, plenty in the midst of lack
Balance in the midst of confusion, gain in the midst of loss
Giving in the midst of greed, courage in the midst of fear
Sharing in midst of selfishness, progress in midst of pathology and freedom in the midst of bondage

Because of him this is what I see
I see the one who reminds me that I can do all things through Christ who strengthens me
Because of him I see heaven in midst of hell,
Victory in the midst of defeat, I see LIFE in midst of death
Because of him this is what I see

****

Whom Shall You Serve? Who Are You Serving?

I'm serving the one that shelters me from the storm and whose spirit speaks to my soul and tells me to look away from the prognosis and focus on the promise.
So I ask ... *Who Are You Serving?* I'm serving a God that tells me that all I have is not all there is

And I'm not working for living; I'm working for a giving.
I'm serving a God that tells me that even though the world tells you—you can't, you shouldn't and you won't; HIS POWER says I can, I should, and by his name I will!

I'm serving a God that tells me there is power in the tongue, thus my circumstances can be affected by the words I speak
So that means I shall give no word power to crashing crises

If I say I'm poor, then poverty shall be my name
If I say I'm broke, then I'll be shattered
If I say I'm sick, then I'll be confined to the bed of infirmity
If I say I'm a failure, then I'll continue to be unsuccessful
If I say my kids are bad, then my kids will be worse
If I say I'm going to die, may God help me for I'm already
dead

For I am the seed of Abraham;
I'm an heir to God's promise to him
Thus according to this Promise I may be:
Hindered but not halted, delayed but not denied
Slowed down, but not stopped
Depressed but not devastated
Paused but not prevented, devalued but not deficient
Captured but not crushed, and lost but not left
Flawed but not failed, impatient but not imprisoned
Weak but not wasted, remiss but never removed

The God I serve teaches me about the difference between
man's faith and God's faith
Man's faith is based on what is before his eyes,
God's faith is based on what's beyond his spirit
So through it all, I may be

Cast out but never conquered
Tested and tortured but never taken
Doubted but never dominated
Alienated but never annihilated
Sentenced but never surrendered
Targeted but not terminated
Bruised, blamed but never bonded
Deserted but never destroyed
Jobless but not joy-less
Foiled but never fatherless

So I ask, Who Are You Serving?
See I serve a master that tells me if you're going to do all that
praying, then why waste your time with all that worrying?
And if you going to do all that worrying;
Then why waste your time with all that praying?

The God I serve teaches me that fear tolerated is faith
contaminated and the best blessing blocking mechanism is to
doubt his unexplainable capabilities
In short, just because folks can't see it,
doesn't mean God can't do it!
I'm serving a God who is good, whose mercies are
everlasting, and whose truth endures to all generations
So I ask, "Who Are You Serving?"

****

Who Am I? I Am Him

Who am I? What am I? I am him the man, the Black Man
Child of the most high.

I am a man who thirsts for knowledge and finds work,
struggle, and prayer no stranger. I am a man who loves to
love and who loves to be loved. I am a man who understands
that life begins, and never ends through the spirit. I am a man
who believes in the equation that says (Balance + Harmony =
Peace) which is the daughter of Love

I am a man who understands the difference between Godly
religion and relationship with God. I am a man who at times
may be misunderstood by man but always understood by
God

Who am I? What am I? I am him the man, the Black Man Child of the most high

I am a man who knows there is no way to intellectualize the miraculous actions of the spirit, and no matter what, in the end God has the last say. I am a man who believes that making a living, and making a life are two totally different things. I am a man who says that when it comes to relationships don't just bring something to the table, bring your own table

I am a man whose spirit is caressed by life's little things; a drive at sunrise, a child's laughter, fabulous fallen autumn leaves, a woman's smile, a smooth warm lake front breeze, and jazz tracks of my choice that have me searching for a moment of prayer and my grandma's voice

I am a man whose grand momma's name is Poetry. She loves and guides me, providing refuge that hides me, she supports me and nurtures me when nature falls short, and she paves the way with words that lead to inner peace

Who am I? What am I? I am him the man, the Black Man Child of the most high
I am a man who believes there is no such thing as bad kids, just bad parents. If you seek a positive child, keep them near positive adults. I am a man who believes that a dysfunctional background is no justification for delinquent and destructive future existence
I am a man who considers himself a BMW in search of the IRS (Black Male and Wonderful and Internal Redemption of Spirit) I am a man who knows your destiny is determined by your words. Your kids will be bad if you call them that; you will remain sick if you keep saying that you are

I am a man who no longer relies on the law buying and selling, but the law sowing and reaping. I can control what I get by focusing on what I give

I am a man who truly believes that Music, Laughter, Poetry and Prayer are the four greatest forms of medicine.
I am a man who believes that failing or falling is not the problem, but the refusal to get up is. Understand, the only thing worse than losing is quitting

I am a man who knows that evil has no particular skin color, gender or nationality, just a deceptive, destructive and demonic personality

I am a man whose greatest assets are the *Four Intangibles* which are: the work of my hands, the passion of my heart, the depth of my mind and the power of my faith

I am a man whose heroes include Jesus, Jessie, Julian, Jarreau,W.E.B Dubois, Jazzman Roy, Harold, Hiram, Haki, Louis, Les, Lena, Langston, Last Poets and Little Rock Nine. Thelonious, Thurgood, Coltrane, Clayton, Carver, and Cornell; Gregory, Gwendolyn, Gil, Gates, Martin Malcolm, Marvin, Marva, Maya, Medgar, Marley Marcus, Miles, Moses, Masons, my brother, and my momma's little man-Me

Who am I? What am I? I am him, the man, the Black Man Child of the most high. I am him

What Is That Spirit?

What is the power of power within what we know as spirit? A spirit dwells about us far beyond abstract thinking and gratuitous claims of understanding. It's the power of spirit, so powerful you can't help but hear it. It's a spirit that will; Makes evil men kind, gives 20/20 vision to the blind, It's a spirit that makes the strongest man weak, makes silent partners attempt to speak, makes the toughest man cry, brings snowfall in the middle of July and compels Mr. Know it All to finally ask, why? What is that Spirit?

It's a spirit that turns pimps into popes while giving the pessimist a sign of hope. It's a spirit that makes bad kids demonstrate proper behavior while making the atheist claim Jesus as the Lord and Savior. It's a spirit that pulls the truth from the biggest liar and takes the North Pole and sets it on fire. It's a spirit that makes it impossible for detectives to find a trace, while convincing the prodigal son to never leave home in the first place. It can spin the earth's rotation into reverse and unlike Superman, it can save the universe

What is that Spirit? It's a spirit that makes Al Sharpton stop rambling, makes riverboat patrons stop gambling, and stops P-Diddy from sampling. It's a spirit that transforms the best from what was once called the worst, makes the devil's disciples disburse, while keeping babies born feet first out of the neighborhood hearse

I speak of the spirit that makes the weaker man the strongest while making the moon, sun and stars fight about which can shine the longest. It's a spirit that takes the addict off drugs, makes professors and prophets out of thugs, a spirit that three times tighter than your grandmother's hugs

What is that Spirit?

****

One Less

I'll be one less.
I'll be one less believing the hype and the lies of someone
else's fantasy trying to become my reality
I'll be one less Black man walking in doubt;
I'll be one less Black man dying to get out
I'll be one less who won't acknowledge God's power,
I'll be less strapped, rolling in the trap in the midnight hour

I'll be one less Black man that you see on the news
in handcuffs with a mug shot, giving momma the blues
I'll be one less Black man living life so sadistic
one less Black man you can call a statistic
I'll be one less Black man running out on his kid
one less brother bragging about a ten year bid

I witness ghost clues left to trap most fools, unable to
properly use life's working tools. I've re-channeled dimes
chills, rhyme drills and cancerous crime skills; shifting over to
the "fighting by writing" will, for I know the void that time
fills
I give God the glory for my story, from midnight till noon
I'll use this poetry as my eulogy in case I die too soon

I'll be one less Blackman fronting like I'm hard
one less dressed in orange and chains walking the prison yard
The state locked many in a cell, so they came out fighting;
but God wrapped me in his love, so I came out writing
My tears serve as ink that flows through my pen,
writing a letter of repentance being for forgiveness of sins

I'm groomed for goodness, grace and greatness

Those who know me can surely attest,
For it was God's will, that I just be still
and become, one less

****

Hip Hop Holocaust (Triple H)

Where were you the day that Hip Hop died?
Its **Hip Hop Holocaust- Hip- Hop- Holler- Cost**
No Mr. *Thug-a-Threat* I see through your lying
Young cats are trying-crying and spying yet denying
tell me is it all just for sport
Nowadays cats are so willing to die,
just to be king of New York.
I'd rather experience God's best,
without getting hacked up, locked up or hurt
I refuse to lose by two shots in the back,
just to be on the front of your homeboy's t-shirt

No Mr. Track master, I like your beat. But what you're
serving with that, I refuse to eat. I can't constantly dwell in
your fantasies of slinging dope and packing heat, allow me to
quickly retreat to a place where Hip Hop is pure;
and like it did in the 80's it served as our community's cure
I now realize it didn't take a rapper from Chicago's South side
to teach me what **Common Sense** is. Years of observation of
death and dope shows me that we need to drop the pop of
hip hop and reach for some Hip-HOPE

Heavy beats and catchy hooks got young babies walking in
lifeless states of hypnosis; bodies moving like fluid while their
minds stay stagnant. Our babies used to be track stars now
they call themselves *Trap Stars*- young potential stars caught

up in the trap, wake me up, pinch me, somebody give me a
slap

Hip- Hop Holocaust

Twenty-eight inch rims, knee high *Tims*, Virginia Slims,
gangster brims, pick ups, trick ups, stick ups, pit bull pups
and diamond encrusted pimp cups. Folks don't say hello
anymore, they just nod and say *"Shortie* what's up?"

No Mr. Record exec. I see what you want and it's not my
respect. You want my mind, my money, and my allegiance
and that monthly check. You want the children to stand on
the corners with hands over hearts saying;

I pledge allegiance, to the *Bling*,
of the united states of platinum chains, iced out grills and all
those useless things
We pledge allegiance to the baller's black hole,
that we descend into with the help of drugs, drinks, drama
and the infamous stripper pole
It's the Hip Hop Holocaust. Triple H. Take a look at how hip
hop has flip flopped and has our babies doing mental
summersaults with no safety net

I see what you want. You want us to buy everything while
owning nothing. You want us to obtain wealth, only to
instantly dump it right back in the economy of this country
You want us to hang in the malls while you dig in the mines
You want us to shine in our mouths rather than shine in our
minds

You want to keep our babies on the corner while you corner
the market. You want our babies to master the streets and
prisons; while you master the corporate sector from which

true wealth and power will derive. I'm not Gloria Gaynor, *but I Will Survive*

You want to keep us entertained with nursery rhymes and catchy cat calls about coon shine dance moves big-booty-balling-gun clap-murder rap-sexual conquests-drug deals, clothes, *crunk*, cars, junk jewelry and other instruments of insurmountable ignorance. Remove us from the *thuggery*, buffoonery, hatred drama and dope;

Let's flip flop the pimp pop and pray for some **Hip Hope**
It's the Hip Hop Holocaust. Triple H.

How far will it go according to your plan Mr. Pay for radio play man? *Does Your Chain Hang Low?*
Why don't you ask my enslaved ancestors about the true length of those chains? This one here doesn't measure twenty inches long, its more like four hundred years long. Can you afford to pay that much? And trust me this chain came with absolutely no ice

From those whips that you lean back and accumulate, to the whips accumulated on the backs of slaves as they leaned over in the hotbed of oppression and hate

What you don't want me to tell them is the truth. You want me to remain silent about the fact that we are witnessing is the manifestation of modern day musical mall minstrel shows laced with cultural genocide via vocal yet voiceless-vilified volunteers; young, starving, system bound soldiers enlisting in the wrong army

It's the Hip Hop Holocaust. Triple H. The overload of *bling, booty-bumping, ballers, baby mammas, banging beats, Benzes, buying the bar, Bentley's, big bills, buck shots* and *burials of bold yet bamboozled Black brothers* has presented a new face that I don't recognize. Now watch as our babies *Lean Back* and *Walk it Out*, shaking their *Laffy Taffy*, with a *Shoulder Lean and Two Step*, *shouting Hey Bay Bay*, as the pied piper of madness leads them down the *platinum brick road* without a heart, a brain, or courage to fight against the true wizard. Hip Hop Holocaust. In efforts to be *hip*, we *hop* over to a land of destruction and devastation, and we hopelessly *holler* at the *cost* of our cultural roots. **Hip-Hop-Holler-Cost**

Click the heels of your Timberlands and Jordan's then pray for deliverance. The wicked witch of the WESTSIDE flies in on her broom of self-destruction and intellectual decay. Your veins are infested with the Triple H dope, I hope the elders can help you cope and refocus the range of your scope and wean you off hip hop and fill you with some Hip Hope

Motivational Ministry

Route 2:
Motivational Ministry

True heroism is remarkably sober, very *non dramatic*. It is not the urge to surpass all others at whatever cost, but the urge to serve others, at whatever cost.

—Arthur Ashe

FABULOUS FIFTEEN KEYS TO SUCCESS

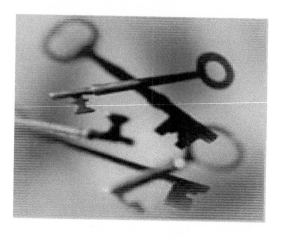

To every person there comes a moment when he is figuratively tapped on the shoulder to do a very special thing unique to him. What a tragedy if that moment finds him unprepared for the work that would be his finest hour.

—Winston Churchill

Are you ready for victory! Are you ready for another way to live life? Are you ready to lean how the manifestation of positive principles can change your life? Are you ready to put prognosis to practice. Are you ready to go from mind to movement? The list below is what I refer to as the **Fabulous Fifteen Keys to Success**. These are fifteen primary points that I have experienced or been taught by experience which can lead to a truly liberating and empowering life. One may see this list and feel the need to add to them; if you feel compelled, do so.

First, I introduce each point to offer a bird's eye view of the keys. In the pages to follow I offer a more in-depth explanation of these points. Some explanations are quite brief and self-explanatory, others require more discussion. Although these keys are pivotal to any reader, I truly had young adults in mind when developing this list.

So if you are the parent of a teenager, I strongly encourage you to share this with them. If you happen to be childless, these principles are very appropriate for application to your life as well. I attest that if you apply these principles to your life, you will begin to experience a victorious and empowering journey through your days. I am not saying one's life will be rid of challenges and trials, but that such challenges can be addressed with less strain and energy than if they were not applied.

FABULOUS FIFTEEN KEYS TO SUCCESS

Don't Be Afraid to Be Different

Surround Yourself with Positive People

Develop Your Mission Statement

Keep God in Your Life

Never Compare Yourself to Others

Listen to Elders; There is Wealth in Their Wisdom

Re-Channel Your Energy/Redirect Your Focus

Sow a Seed

Commit Your Life to Knowledge

Plan "B" Is Not Recommended: It's Required

Do Not Fear Challenge and Change

Watch Your Mouth

"Cool and Cute" Won't Cut It

It's Not About You!

Walk In Victory!

Life isn't about
finding yourself.
Life is about
creating yourself.

—George Bernard
Shaw

Key I: Don't Be Afraid To Be Different

Originality is the birthplace of commonality.
                                        —A.J. Bryson

We currently live during a time where it is effortless and painless just to fit in. Originality has truly lost its splendor. Everything existing in the American culture is a replica of something else. Influence is healthy and admirable, but the extensive level of blatant reproduction of anything desirable poses a true problem.

People have become so consumed in reproducing the identity of others that many of us do not know who we really are. Everyone wants to look alike, talk alike, pursue the same dreams, drive the same car and wear the same clothes. External definition has become the nemesis of original thought, identity and choice.

It is at this point where the cliché' statement, think outside the box, no longer means originality. We no longer need to think outside the box, **we need our own box**, and a much bigger one at that. Our own container of individual imagination and spiritual essence is what we are in dire need of. Many of our young people today have neither inspiration nor an example of a "healthy" sense of originality. Thus they are defined by external forces such as media images and pop culture. The aforementioned tell our youth what to like, what to love, what to hate, what to admire, what to respect, what to ignore, what to eat, what to learn, what to buy, how to live, and how to die. I must also note that the parents of these children are being externally defined as well.

It is only when we can truly shape our own identities, that we will truly have any sense of self-liberation. The majority of truly successful people in this world have done something so different that no one would ever expect it, suspect it, nor be willing to try it first.

Originality and individual creative thought is healthy yet neither praised nor rewarded on large scales. Deciding to do something original or to do something in a manner that's never been done before is essential in attaining success.

Key II: Surround Yourself with Positive People

Psalm 133:1 How good and pleasant it is when brothers live together in unity.

This is very important but many times difficult for some to do. Minister Joel Osteen speaks of an interaction with people involving deposits and withdrawals. People who are around you who are loving, supportive, nurturing, protective, and instructional all add deposits to your life. These individuals add to your life circle by depositing good things in dealing with you on a day-to-day basis.

These individuals go above and beyond to express to you how much you are loved. They tell you how smart, attractive, driven, brilliant, and ambitious you are and how they appreciate your person. These individuals can range from spouses, siblings, friends, colleagues, bosses, parents, children, neighbors, lovers to even total strangers on the morning bus ride.

They offer instruction, inspiration, motivation, support, prayers, blessings, well wishes, favor, compliments, compassion, hugs, advice, smiles, and a listening ear. They offer these things because they truly value you in their lives and they feel fortunate to be a part of yours.

Consequently, there are individuals who are in direct contrast to the aforementioned. There are individuals who make withdrawals on your life. They have a vicious habit of doing or saying things that drain your energy, cloud your judgment, crush your dreams, antagonize your spirit and belittle your accomplishments to say the very least.

The painful reality is that these individuals can also range from spouses, siblings, friends, colleagues, bosses, parents, children, neighbors, lovers, to even total strangers on the morning bus ride. They offer: destructive criticism, hateful wishes, snide remarks, rude gestures, selfish actions, condescending remarks, cold shoulders, comments of disapproval, mockery, envy, judgmental opinions and poisonous perspectives.

The key here is to be ultra-selective about the company you keep. Surround yourself as much as humanly possible with individuals who will make healthy deposits into your life. These are the individuals who say, "Great job, you can do it!" "That's a great idea." etc. I speak not of finding folks to stroke ones ego, but those who are genuinely dedicated to your advancement.

Key III: Develop Your Mission Statement

Proverbs 29:18 Where there is no vision the people perish.

Nearly every major corporation, service institution and non-for profit organization has a well-developed and highly revered mission statement. We must understand that there is a difference between a goal and a mission statement. A goal speaks about a generic nonspecific result or outcome. A mission statement not only introduces the desired result or outcome, but it goes steps further and discusses specific targeted population and reasons why the result or outcome is desired. A mission statement is a constant reminder of what the initial goals are.

Many may think that mission statements are only for groups, systems or corporations. This is not so. Each individual who desires success and who desires to help others should have a mission statement for their lives.

For example, what is your mission statement as a single parent? It should include developing more than just your child? Your mission statement as a college student should include more than just getting your degree. Your mission statement as a member of your church should include more than just your church and it members. Your mission statement as an employee should include more than just your promotion. Please note that, YOUR JOB IS YOUR DUTY AND ASSIGMENMENT BUT NOT YOUR MISSION!

A mission statement speaks about a substantial need or lack of something and the particular good or service of the company (or yourself) is what will be provided to fill that need or eradicate that lack. A mission statement is good for any individual or institution.

Reverend Greg Blair of Chicago speaks of mission statements as he provides premarital counseling to engaged couples. He charges each couple he counsels to develop a mission statement for their marriage. It provides a clear and definite path for what married couples plan to accomplish as husband and wife. This is all about the concept of sharing your blessing. His reasons for the mission statement involve a married couple being more that just being a married couple. What affect will their marriage have on others?

In being successful one must develop a game plan, a schematic, a blueprint, a target audience, and a demonstrated lack that one hopes to fulfill. This is what is known as your *Mission Statement* which also asserts that there is a gift to give.

*What is your gift?

A mission is not only a goal or desire, it's a commitment. Each of us developing our mission statement must recognize our gift. We each have a gift and God wants us to use that gift wisely. To elaborate further on the concept of God-given gifts, I reference the words of a talented aspiring minister. LeRoy Brown Jr. the creator of *Fresh Manna for Today* internet ministry offers the comparison of God's gifts to an actual pregnancy as he asks the question:
Will You Carry Full-Term?

"In these last two and a half months I've realized the importance of carrying a baby full term. To carry a baby full term is to be pregnant for 37 to 40 weeks. I've learned a baby that is born full-term has a better chance of survival, compared to a baby born prematurely. It is through the development (pregnancy) stage, the baby is given all of the nutrients and supplements necessary for optimal health, growth and development.

Similarly, <u>God has impregnated you with a gift</u>. Are your gifts in the developmental stage or are you about to give birth? God has and will give you everything necessary for your gift to go forth into the world. He is waiting for your gift to be delivered. Don't allow the devil to cause you to have a miscarriage or make you question your gift and abort it. The devil wants your gift before it's delivered. Stay focused! Be humble! Know that the delivery or manifestation of your gift will bring you and others victory."

James 1:17 Every good gift and every perfect gift is from above, and comes down from the father of lights with whom there is no variation or shadow of turning.

So as you ponder what your mission statement will be, consider these specific things:

* What is your gift, service or talent that you will offer society?

* Can you speak about the demonstrated need for your gift?

* Who will your target audience be? Who will receive the greatest benefit from what you will offer?

71

* What is your desired outcome of providing your gift?

* How do you plan to deliver or distribute your gift?

In summation; the mission statement offers more than just a stated goal. It gives your life an assignment of purpose by executing your plan and distributing your gift.

Key IV: Keep God in Your Life
(Not Religion but Relationship)

Proverbs 3:6 In all thy ways acknowledge him, and he shall direct thy paths.

This actually should have been key number one. Anyone over the age of twelve can assert that life will throw challenges and trials toward you. One can find themselves in a position requiring a lot more than help from man.

I am of the belief that a spiritual connection is needed in order to live life in abundance and freedom. Our ancestors knew that in order for our generation to make it this far, we would need assistance, favor, blessings, mercy and grace of a higher power. Everyone from African kings and queens to soldiers of the civil rights movement knew that success in their causes and victory in their battles could not have been possible without the hand of God.

I speak not of specific religion, but more so a "relationship" and true spiritual connection with God.
Having that much needed spiritual connection is the foundation and driving force behind the aforementioned

mission statement. When such a spiritual connection is established, it calms the fears of those who depend entirely too much on the efforts of man. The bible states that *God did not give us the spirit of fear, but that of love and a sound mind.* (2 Timothy 1:7) Your spirit must remain fearless through your faith.

Understanding that spiritual connection gives you only optimism in the midst of earthly panic. Stock market crashes, poor economy, layoffs, are just a few things that cause the average American to panic severely. The grace and mercy of God provides a calm spirit and motivation to serve others, which I will address later.

I have been in positions where I have been laid off from my job. I was disappointed but not devastated for I knew God would provide a greater opportunity for me. Fellow coworkers gave me greetings of pity such as, "I'm so sorry, what are you going to do now? I can't believe this is happening!" If not for my faith in God, I would have panicked in similar fashion to my coworkers.

Understand that when you are strong in your faith and understand the power of God, you see that your job was just your duty, not your source. So as man closes one door, God opens another.
Understanding that God is your source and will provide your needs, gives you a sense of freedom where you don't worry about firings, layoffs, difficult bosses, or co-workers. One with strong faith believes; just as God has provided you with the blessings of the past, blessings of the future are inevitable.

It is only with serious faith that one can truly manifest my previous assertion. Many individuals claim they have faith but have difficulty exercising it during challenging times. It is not my position to gauge your individual faith, but to express to you that strong faith is the ultimate shield against fear. As expressed earlier, "A tolerated fear is a contaminated faith."

Minister LeRoy Brown of or Fresh Manna Ministries discusses this in his question: **"Religion or Relationship: Which one will you choose?"**

"More often than not, many of us confuse being religious with having a relationship with God. Religion may teach us doctrine. However; a relationship with God shows us who we really are. While religion may give us an experience with God, having a relationship with Him gives us purpose and allows us the opportunity to fulfill our destiny.

Have you been looking for a religious experience instead of a life long relationship? Well, it is time to seek a relationship with God. A relationship fosters intimacy that leads to true love. Commit yourself to a long lasting relationship with God.

Your religion may have introduced you to God, but it is your relationship with Him that will sustain your love. When we decide to seek a relationship with God our hearts will be filled with true joy, love and happiness."

Having a strong relationship with God brings peace to your heart, revelation to your mind, power to your life, and meaning to your existence.

Key V: Never Compare Yourself to Others

I spent years of my life trying to be like them, only to find out they spent those same years trying to be like me.

—Author Unknown

This is one of the most common mistakes we make in our lives and actually one of the most difficult to avoid. Comparison to others is done subconsciously; therefore, many times we have no idea of what's taking place. You are an individual uniquely created. You are something that no one else will ever be. What must be understood is that constantly comparing ourselves to others gives us an unrealistic and unbalanced view of ourselves. When we compare ourselves to others either one of two things will occur. We will suffer from low self-esteem or develop a tremendous sense of arrogance. I'll use the examples of two friends of mine.

My first friend (let's call her Heather) is an outgoing, vibrant, intelligent, and attractive young woman. However, Heather constantly displays intimidation when other women enter the room. She is always comparing her qualities to theirs (in a negative way). Heather frequently sees other women as always "more" than she is; using everything from hair length, complexion, height, weight body shape to occupations of other women to make her feel as though she will never match up.

Celebration of one's self removes the need to compare with others. If Heather decided to celebrate her own achievements, qualities, body shape, complexion, occupation etc., she would have neither time nor thought to mentally beat herself down by focusing on what she doesn't have. One danger in comparing yourself to others is that you risk feeling that you will never measure up.

My next friend (let's call him Jordan) is the total opposite of Heather. Jordan is a successful and outgoing guy that's involved with everything. He's what you would call, "Mr. In Crowd." Jordan frequently compares himself to others as well.

However, different from Heather, his comparisons are with those individuals less than or who may be living undesirable lifestyles. With his comparisons, Jordan feels superior and often looks down on others in a very condescending manner. Jordan compares himself to prisoners, deadbeat dads, criminals, abusive husbands, pedophile priests, alcoholics, unscrupulous politicians, etc. Doing this makes Jordan feel that he is above others due to the fact that his life doesn't mirror theirs.

This type of comparison gives Jordan a false sense of superiority over other individuals that he chooses to compare himself to. Similar to Heather's "I'm not enough" attitude, Jordan's is also unhealthy because his attitude carries an arrogance that says "they are so beneath me."

So I implore you to make a concerted effort to never compare yourself to the progress or downfall of others. If you are not careful you will find yourself never measuring up, or feeling others can never measure up to you. Such arrogance can be toxic. You should always maintain confidence but balance it with humility. Having that balance will compel you to be grateful for what you have, but always be willing to help and pray for those who aren't where you are.

Key VI: Listen to Elders. There is Wealth in Their Wisdom

Proverbs 11:14   Where there is no cause, the people fall. But in the multitude of counselors there is safety.

1 Peter 5:5 Likewise you younger people, submit yourselves to your elders.

This is one of the most underrated forms of advice one can ever receive. Innovative technology, pop culture juxtaposed with cutting edge perspectives on what's hip and cool, all have pulled many of us away from the dinner table of good old-fashioned conventional wisdom. The discussion involving two people on a back porch with a glass of lemonade has all but disappeared in our modern world. People reach the status of elders for a reason. It resonates that years of living well has brought forth a harvest of wisdom. It takes a great deal of humility and patience to acquire information given from the elders. The delivery of information may be different and not the most glamorous; however, the information remains incredibly valuable.

The elders of our community hold a vault of life changing secrets, mantras and proverbs and they are eager to pass them on. It is up to the youth to take the time and energy necessary to pursue this wisdom. Grandparents, parents, clergy members, seasoned community leaders, scholars, educators and business owners are just a few individuals that are referred to as elders. Do you realize that many civilizations thrived, flourished, and prospered because of their ability to manifest the advice and wisdom of their elders? The transferal of culture, language, customs and philosophy takes place between the exchange of youth and elder. Find that jewel that is the wisdom of those that precede us.

Key VII: Re-Channel Your Energy/Redirect Your Focus

Romans 12:2 Be not conformed to this word but be ye transformed by the renewal of your mind.

We all have several talents and energies that just need to be redirected in a constructive manner. We have talents of memory, solution finding, information distribution, and resource location and inspiration delivery. These are just a few areas that we exercise on a daily basis and are unaware that we can utilize these everyday talents to make substantial contributions in our lives as well as the lives of others.

When I speak to students ranging from 5th graders to college interns, the message is the same and this very principal conveniently applies. Success in school comes down to two basic rules, **one, work hard**, and **two, re-channeling your energy**. If students can memorize hundreds of songs they hear on the radio, then they should be able to memorize things that apply to schoolwork. Theories, formulas and rules of writing are things applicable to schoolwork that can be memorized if a student's energy is re-channeled.

A good friend of mine is a middle school teacher (we'll call her Ms. Coke) who uses the "re-channeled energy" approach to helping her students learn in the classroom. I witnessed once as I sat in her class how she taught her seventh grade students ways to remember the Preamble to the U.S Constitution. Ms. Coke was intrigued (but not surprised) at how they could recite numerous lyrics of songs by artist ranging from Jay Z and Kanye West, to Alicia Keys and Mary J Blige.

Ms. Coke took a survey of popular songs that she heard them singing throughout the day and listened to melodies, harmonies, and rhythms. She then took the words to the preamble and fused them within these rhythmic melodies from the songs the students were singing.

At first it seemed a bit ambitious and labor intensive. However, as the students were introduced to the mode of memorization and learning via familiar rhythms, they were floored by their own ability to learn so quickly. Shortly after, it was revealed that students in Ms. Coke's class were more proficient in memorization of various areas than every other class in the school. The preamble was just the beginning. They applied this approach to English, math, and science concepts as well. The principal was impressed and fellow teachers were amazed and/or jealous of her efforts.

What was witnessed in Ms. Coke's class was a re-channeling of energy and redirection of focus. Students took the energy and focus they used on memorizing popular songs and re-channeled/redirected that towards learning in the classroom.

Initially as Ms. Coke explained to them that they could in fact learn different concepts just as easy as they learned popular songs, the students were not sold. For they felt the fact they heard songs frequently throughout the day was the explanation for effortless memorization. But the point they made but missed was "repetition." Sometimes repetition is involuntary, sometimes it isn't. She explained if they made the effort to include such concepts within their daily routines, they would find that regular frequency helpful.

They saw learning as more enjoyable because they used their everyday informal talents and applied them to something more formal. Needless to say, Ms. Coke has received praise, awards, and citywide honors for her efforts. The students in Ms. Coke's class re-channeled their energy and re-directed their focus.

Key VIII: Sow a Seed

Luke 6:38 Give and it shall be given unto you, good measured, pressed down, shaken together and running over shall men give unto your bosom.

It's something we have all heard before. Many call it the *Law of the Harvest, i.e., sowing and reaping*. What I have found throughout many life experiences is that you affect what you receive by paying close attention to what you give. What you put out comes back to you. If you want to receive the best you must give the best. Understand that this goes far beyond what you will hear your local minister discuss in

80

reference to tithes and offerings. Sowing a seed is a figurative assertion as well as it is a natural order.

As you make contributions to the lives of others, those very contributions are returned in one way or another. Take for instance parents who care about their school systems and are truly involved with local officials. These parents make substantial contributions that can be returned in the face of improved conditions of that school.

In these improved schools, the students are positively affected and they grow to become prosperous, intelligent contributors to society. These schools may in fact produce the next powerful educator, entrepreneur, clergy person, civic leader or world-changing artist.

Corporations that make charitable contributions and provide volunteers to help certain causes may be repaid by an increase in advertising, which can lead to increased profits. Homeowners, who care greatly not only for their property, but their entire neighborhood, sow seeds of community development.

Whether it is community activities, rules about property appearance, neighborhood watch and beautification efforts; all of these are seeds sown by neighborhood residents that will produce a harvest of a more attractive environment. Consequently, this may increase their property value and make more families desire to live in that particular area, once again demonstrating a return on investment if you will. This is basically reaping and sowing.

In reference to monetary seed sowing, Reverend Greg Blair of Deep Thought Ministries in Chicago offers the following statement:

"When we give to God, He will give unto us. God wants to make us (God financiers). One way that He does this is through our giving. When we give, we are allowing God to supply others needs through us. God will make us his (money warehouses) when we let his giving move us to give. We need to get God off the charity list and put him on the payroll. We need to make our giving to God a habit and not an occasional event. A lot of people are willing to give God the credit, but not too many are willing to give him cash. We make a living by what we get, but we make a life by what we give. Remember, what you give lives!"

Although seed sowing includes this, it also extends far beyond making any financial contribution to a cause, movement, or ministry. It is basically making deposits into the lives of individuals which may enhance the quality of life. Sowing seeds also includes intangible yet meaningful contributions. Another example is someone who is a tax expert may volunteer to do free tax services for those who cannot afford a tax preparer or who may not know how to do their own. Those who are human resources professionals can aid others in creating and developing strong resumes and cover letters and possibly give advice on interview etiquette. Former sports players can volunteer their wisdom of the game to young aspiring athletes via coaching a little league team.

Personal fitness trainers can volunteer and show children and adults exercise routines that can keep them healthy. Former models and fashion experts can help develop community fashion seminars helping young people to see their dreams in the fashion industry. Law enforcement officers can aid in community meeting by instructing residents on how to keep their neighborhoods safe. Church members can visit hospital patients or incarcerated individuals offering prayer and conversation.

Many times I find myself speaking at schools for their professional career day, read aloud celebration, *Real Men Read* program, poetry slams, Black history month program, rites of passage rituals, or judging oratorical contests; strictly on a volunteer basis. When you sow seeds into children, there is a harvest of hope and potential in that child.

My purpose for speaking extensively on this is to demonstrate that sowing a seed far exceeds writing a check or dropping money into the church collection plate. Though I do sow monetary seeds, I felt compelled to provide the aforementioned as examples of seed sowing that do not require monetary donations. Examine the following list of things you can impart on someone's life:

love, admiration, concern, support, friendship, prayer, companionship, instruction, leadership, inspiration, devotion, opportunity, wisdom, praise, compassion, sympathy, sincerity, favor, good-will, forgiveness, laughter, direction, guidance, protection, and even discipline

When you provide the aforementioned things, you make substantial deposits into the lives of others. Making these deposits can be interpreted as sowing seeds. Things included on the list above serve as clear-cut examples of seeds sown into our daily existence. Those who impart things such as these provide a tremendous benefit to the lives of those they touch.

Thus, I strongly encourage you to focus on what you give because it will directly affect what you will get. When we take substantial efforts to make contributions into the lives of others, these efforts don't go unnoticed. They are returned to us as blessings and favor. I firmly believe that your business, your family, career, relationships, aspirations, needs and creative ideas will flourish because of your seed sowing. Every good seed adds to your harvest. So I implore you, regardless of the type, SOW A SEED!

Key IX: Commit Your Life to Knowledge

Proverbs 23:12 Apply your heart to instruction and your ears to words of knowledge.

Hosea 4:6 My people are destroyed for lack of knowledge.

True education enrolls people at the cradle and graduates them at the grave. I first heard this statement at a commencement ceremony and thought it to be very profound and intriguing because it spoke volumes of truth. Education and learning is a process that extends from our birth to death. Each day we are alive, an opportunity to learn and gain wisdom presents itself. If we are to live a life of fulfillment, liberation and victory, we cannot dismiss the need for continued learning.

Learning is the food that we feed our selves to sustain us for our duties. Just as one feeds their bodies to have strength to carry out physical duty, our minds must constantly feed in order to have adequate intellectual nourishment.

Regardless of how many accolades, awards, degrees and praise we receive for what we know, there is always much more to learn. What we must understand is that the incredible thing about knowledge is that it is never-ending. I believe this was God's plan for knowledge and education so that no man could truly say *he knows all.* The most highly revered and prestigious faculty members at America's universities all share one common goal; to learn more than what they previously knew. For they realize that PhD does not stand for *Put History Down,* but learning about the past and examining the present compels true educators to seek answers to our future.

The quest for knowledge is what makes some individuals awake each morning. This is my hope for everyone that reads this book. It is my hope that you awake each morning asking, "What more can I learn today? What will I learn today that I never knew before?"

What we must understand is that education is not only for consumption, it is also to be used to ask new questions and create new knowledge. If we all consumed the knowledge of this world without adding to that knowledge, we would experience an arrested development.

In high school and college, students are taught to acquire knowledge; however in graduate and professional schools, students are charged to create that knowledge.

Someone has to create new ways to teach, new ways to learn, and new ways to serve. Those who continue to seek further knowledge in part bring upon the advancements of modern society. That knowledge is (at times) put into products, goods and services that help our society to live a better life. This is the regenerative essence of education. It creates individuals with the capacity to seek further truth and knowledge.

Key X: Plan "B" Is Not Recommended, It's Required

What a tragedy it is for a man to put all his hopes and dreams in one basket, only to find that his dream basket has a hole in the bottom. **–AJ Bryson**

It is imperative to anyone who wishes for satisfaction in life to have a plan B. In this case, I'll say that B stands for "Back Up." We all have something that we desire or wish for ourselves whether it is a particular career, college major, choice of neighborhood, business plan, or route to work.

Having a back up plan provides you a second option that could be life changing. You may find in life that what you originally planned or pursued may not have come to fruition. It is in those times that it is imperative to have something that you can find refuge and fulfillment in.

From the age of nine years old I have always wanted to be a professional football player. That was my dream; my big brother also held that same dream, and it was my father's ultimate dream for the both of us. I played little league, high school and a year of college football with diligence, devotion, conviction, and unspeakable commitment. I ate, drank and even slept holding a football.

As most young athletes do, in high school I convinced myself that I was good enough to actually compete at the next level. Consequently, after a knee injury in college and a "tall glass of reality," I realized my football playing days were numbered. I was forced to choose another dream. Fortunately, I was blessed enough to have a back up plan for my life. I felt empowered because leaving the game of football didn't leave me with feelings of emptiness and meaningless. I simply interpreted it as the end of one chapter and the start of the next.

Thus, I strongly encourage you to develop a second sight. When I speak to young athletes, the furthest thing from their minds is NOT making it to the NFL or NBA. They are so hopeful and confident in their abilities that not making it to the professional ranks never enters their minds. For it is here that I become the proverbial "Grinch" by telling these young men not what they want to hear, but <u>what they need to hear</u>.

I charged them to pursue the NFL and NBA with much zeal and vigor. However, I spoke to them candidly about developing as many skills off the court as they have developed on the court. I encouraged them to not only be the **(B.M.O.C) Big Man on Campus,** but to also become the **Big Man of the Corporation** or the **Big Man of the Cause.** I realize this was no pep talk but it's "Real Talk." It is my belief that when young adults truly understand this concept, they become better equipped to deal with the unpredictable nature of life's circumstances.

As I speak to parents of these athletes, I strongly encouraged them to highlight and focus on their child's academic triumphs as well as the athletic ones. I asked them, "What are you teaching your child that will make them marketable in the event that sports are not in their occupational future?"

Just as young people need to establish a plan B for their lives, parents must not cripple their child with a "mono directional" game plan. Parents should encourage variety and diversity in the planning of their children's lives. We all need a reserve in everything we do. One never knows, there may actually be refuge in the reserve.

So as you read this tenth key ask yourself the following:

1. Have I established what my plan B actually is?

2. If I can't do my number one choice of occupation what else will I do?

3. Have I acquired the knowledge and talents necessary that will keep me successful in the event that my first choice doesn't work?

4. What are other things that I enjoy and am good at that could result in a fulfilling and successful career?

Plan to prepare yourself for the unexpected. Grooming yourself for greatness has to involve a variety of talents strengths and experience. Having a plan B could just wind up being your plan A.

Key XI: Do Not Fear Challenge and Change

2 Timothy 1:7 God did not give us the spirit of fear, but that of love and a sound mind.

It is pretty much a certainty that challenges and obstacles will arise in your life. I've learned that character is built not by what happens to you, but how you adjust and overcome your circumstances. There are many people who are simply frightened to reach for their dreams because they fear failure rejection and insensitivity. Success is an outfit that only fits those with thick skin.

We must not accept the word "NO," but just be able to look beyond it in hopes for the YES moment. The closing of one door is just a message to say that there are many other doors potentially open. But if you are devastated by the closing of that one door, you may stifle your ability to locate the other doors that may provide so much more. If there is a dream you want to accomplish, you must be devoted and not be worrisome about what others may think or say. Do not fear the word no, or listen to others who feel that what you plan to do is a waste of time. Challenges and tribulations may arise, but what is important for us to know is that we are all blessed in a special way. And if God's blessing is upon you, you have no need to fear.

When I decided to write this book, I experienced the naysayer who said it wouldn't work because no one likes poetry and poetry doesn't' sell like novels. I was told that the book wouldn't be sold beyond family and friends who would make mercy purchases. In addition, there were various challenges with logistics, time, resources as well as my own efforts and imagination to see the project through.

Part of the reason we fear challenges and change is because of past failures. We cannot allow what happened years ago to affect our new search for success. Again I reference Rev. Greg Blair of *Deep Thought Ministries* as he offers this profound assertion:

Don't Look Back. "Have you ever driven a car by looking through the rear view mirror? While you wouldn't think of driving in such a manner, many of us are living our lives that way. We are living our lives by looking at the past. That is why we sometimes "run into" problems because our attention and focus are somewhere else. If we keep looking at past mistakes, old regrets and missed opportunities, we can never see what God has for us now."

"We are always led by what we focus our attention on. If we focus on the past, we will keep making the same mistakes over and over. When we keep our eyes on the future, we will begin to see new opportunities to enrich our lives. Let the past go. It is over and done with. What is done is done. Forgive all those old people, places and things and move on. Today, let us keep our eyes on the future. Let us forgive and let us forget the past. When we make peace with our past, our future will be ready to open its arms to us. It's a new day!"

In addition, prepare yourself for an exodus from your comfort zone. You will have to be around people that you've never been around before, unveil thoughts that you've only kept to yourself, and go places you never thought you would go. The change in environment can be healthy in helping one not only find a sense of home, but to make wherever you go home in itself. Understand that when striving for success, happiness, and victory in life, it's not about comfort and convenience, but about character and commitment.

Key XII: Watch Your Mouth

Proverbs 18:21 The tongue has the power of life and death, and those who love it will eat its fruit.

Proverbs 13:3 He who guards his mouth preserves his life, but he who opens wide his lips shall have destruction.

Proverbs 15:4 The tongue that brings healing is a tree of life, but a deceitful tongue crushes the spirit.

To combat verbal ridicule as children, we were taught the mantra "Sticks and stones may break my bones, but words will never hurt me." We need to go back and rewrite the words to say something more like, ***Sticks and stones may break your bones, but words control your destiny...*** Words are powerful. Understand that words are spirits dressed in sound, and are conductors or heartfelt energy that put forth action of a particular circumstance. What you speak comes from your heart; and what is in your heart speaks volumes to where you may be headed in your life.

Our words must be carefully selected as we plan to strive for fulfillment. Fulfillment and success in life does not only come from dreams, ambitions, and thoughts. What is spoken plays a very substantial part in where we go in life.

Words represent data which is sent to our brain that instructs us to carry out certain functions. While in graduate school, I witnessed senior level doctoral students calling each other Dr. Thomson, Dr. Smith Dr. Anderson or Dr. *(insert your name)*.

They had not yet graduated or received their Ph.D's but they spoke as if they were already professors. These graduate students didn't see themselves as they were at the time; they saw themselves as how they would be. They repeatedly called themselves doctor because that's where they saw themselves, even though they had not yet crossed the commencement threshold. They literally and figuratively spoke to their future.

That same action applies to us as well. As we groom ourselves for greatness, speaking to that success daily is as recommended as a multi-vitamin and eight glasses of water. Each morning when we look in the mirror, we must speak positive energy into our lives. We must tell ourselves (everyday) we are beautiful, smart, healthy, wealthy, creative, valuable, talented, brilliant, worthy, and blessed. I do not mean brag on yourself in an arrogant manner. I am simply speaking to you addressing yourselves in a positive, empowering, motivational and constructive way. Say to yourself, this is the day that I do something great!

People do not get paid to praise value or uplift you. More times than often we are surrounded by jealous, envious, spiteful and indifferent individuals who make more withdrawals with their words than deposits. We can effortlessly find ourselves around people daily, who tell us that we are not pretty enough, smart enough, talented enough, rich enough, or connected enough. It is at these times that we must guard ourselves from all negativity with daily affirmations about ourselves. Speak to your success daily!

* Don't be hung by your tongue!

Just as I encourage you to speak words of construction motivation and productivity, I implore you to avoid negative talking. Avoid the *doubt route* containing words of doubt fear, sickness, poverty and even death. In informal conversation we speak words that we truly don't believe in our hearts. Let's examine some of the phrases we use in normal daily conversation that speak opposite of what we really desire.

- ❖ That was so funny I almost <u>died </u>laughing.
- ❖ I've been walking all day and my feet are <u>killing</u> me.
- ❖ I'm <u>afraid</u> I won't be able to make it.
- ❖ They play that song so much that it makes me <u>sick</u>.
- ❖ This job is going to be the <u>death of me.</u>
- ❖ We're selling so much we're going to <u>make a killing.</u>

Do we really wish to be sick, afraid, and dead or to even kill someone? It becomes imperative that we are mindful in our choice of words that speak to death, fear, murder, sickness and poverty. If you are hearing such an argument for the first time, my assertions may sound somewhat absurd. As some individuals read this they are probably saying "okay he's getting too deep with this, my goodness they are just harmless words."

They may actually seem like "just words" that don't hurt anyone, but understand what your words do. Our words speak to our hearts and minds about how we perceive circumstances. In addition, words are verbal seeds. The words you speak may either add blessings to your heart or poison it. Here is another way to examine my statements, let's call it the *Words to Destiny Schematic*:

Watch your words, they become your thoughts.
Watch your thoughts, they become your emotions.
Watch your emotions, they become your decisions.
Watch your decisions, they become your actions.
Watch your actions, they become your habits.
Watch your habits, they become your character.
Watch your character, it becomes your destiny.

We have not because we speak not! This serves as a figurative map about the relationship between our destiny and our words. The starting gate is represented by our words and the finish line is represented by our destiny and in between is a culmination of our thoughts, emotions, decisions, actions, and habits. I believe if we can frame our minds to watch our words and follow the *Words to Destiny Schematic* we will be on our way to incredible change and empowerment. Lastly, I want to demonstrate how the *Words to Destiny Schematic* works in reverse as well.

If you don't like your destiny, change your character.
If you don't like your character, change your habits.
If you don't like your habits, change your actions.
If you are unhappy with your actions, change your decisions.
If you are unhappy with your decisions, change your emotions.
If you are unhappy with your emotions, change your thoughts.

Finally, if you are unhappy with your thoughts, you must change your words. Words are seeds that are planted in the hearts and minds of every individual. Positive destinies begin with positive words. Speak to your destiny!

Key VIII: "Cool and Cute" Won't Cut It

Isaiah 2:11 The eyes of the arrogant man will be humbled and the pride of men brought low; the LORD alone will be exalted in that day.

This point addresses those individuals who are relying on their looks and or smooth demeanor as a way to advance in life. As kids, cool and cute were nice attributes to have. As we mature into adults, we witness individuals who use the two simply as a shield for their inadequacy. I explain to young people that at an early age it's easy to be cool and cute. However, as people enter the culture of the real word, you may find yourself in an environment where everyone is cool and cute. Or you just may find yourself in an environment where nobody is cool or cute. What else can you offer? What talents and gifts do you have that are marketable?

In either case you will have to possess some admirable characteristic that supersedes being cool and cute. You will have to perform, show and prove, or basically "walk the walk." Some individuals are admired so much for being cool and cute through the early years of their lives that when adulthood arrives, they have no other skill than being cool and cute. Thus, they are left in a dangerous and dependant state. In addition, in many cases arrogance and pride seem to become common among individuals who rely on being cool and cute.

I Peter 5: 5-6 For God resists the proud, but gives grace to the humble

Anyone who returns to their ten or twenty year high school reunion can attest that some of the coolest and cutest students in their senior class are now neither cute nor cool. Groom yourself for greatness in a holistic manner so that you will not have to depend on being cool or cute.

An individual has not
started living until he can
rise above the narrow
confines of his
individualistic concerns to
the broader concerns of all
humanity.

—Dr. Martin Luther King, Jr.

Key XIV: It's Not About You!

John 3:16 For God so loved the world that he gave his only begotten son so that whosoever believeth in him should not perish but have everlasting life.

Philippians 2:4 Each of you should look not only to your own interests, but also to the interests of others.

Proverbs 27:2 Let another praise you, and not your own mouth; someone else, and not your own lips.

IT'S NOT ABOUT YOU. I used three bible scriptures to support and speak to the sincerity of this phrase. This phrase consists of four simple words with a meaning so powerful and profound; yet, it turns most people completely off. Many hear this phrase and immediately become offended. How dare someone say that it's not about you—why the nerve of them! When I speak at commencement ceremonies, proud parents look at me with scowls, scorn, disapproval and disbelief when I say boldly to their precious little ones that *"It's Not About You."* However, after I present a full explanation of what I meant by that phrase, I am met with agreement, affirmation, and applause.

References to previous key numbers *eight* and *nine* discuss this in their own way. It is my belief that when individuals truly manifest this statement of selflessness, community development, harmony, peace, and society advancement are inevitable. In our society we are taught that life should be all about us. We uplift and praise ourselves even at the expense and downfall of others. We focus on ourselves and ourselves only. Look at the phrases commonly used in our culture:

* It's a dog eat dog world
* Every man for himself
* Us four and no more
* Survival of the fittest
* I've got mine, now you get yours

Our culture perpetuates a social structure of systematic selfishness. We have abandoned previous noted phrases such as:

* Am I my brother's keeper?
* It takes a village to raise a child
* Share the wealth
* Each one teach one
* Women and children first

As you read the above statements you may agree that it's disheartening at times looking at the daily operations of our world. I propose the following questions:

* Who are we claming as brothers and are we really keeping them?
* What happened to the village that once raised the child but now abuses them?
* What are we sharing that is truly beneficial?
* Who is benefiting from what we have learned?
* Who are we teaching or more importantly *what* are we teaching?
* Why does it seem that women and children are the most common victims of our society's ills of today?

What is meant by this phrase? This phrase implies that all that you are, all that you acquire, all that you learn and all that you cultivate is meant for one purpose. **That purpose is to enrich the lives of others**. It is imperative to understand that God's vision for man is not to dwell in this world selfishly. The enrichment and harmony of our society is based on a cooperative existence. In short, we must all work together for the benefit of one another. We are responsible for the care and well being of each other. "Yes, I am my brother's keeper." So when you truly comprehend this phrase you must come to the realization that it's not about you or—

Your status-your car-your family name-your good looks-your heritage-your neighborhood-your wealth-your educational degree-your upbringing-your political connections-your wedding-your separation-your divorce-your feelings-your heartaches-your appearance-your reputation-your occupational title-your new boyfriend/girlfriend-your political party-your circle of friends-your dinner plans-your accomplishments-your weekend plans or vacation-your salary-your organizational memberships-your-wardrobe-your past experiences-your wisdom-your age-your to-do list-your appointment schedule-or your collection of trinkets of status and wealth.

It's not even about the very book you are reading right now. It's fundamentally about the questions that ask:
* What are **you** going to do to bless someone else's child?
* What are **you** going to do to ensure that someone's life is positively affected by something you have done, said or demonstrated?
* What contributions will **you** make to someone's life that will make today better than yesterday, but only half as good as tomorrow?

It is more than evident that most of us are where we are today because of historical seeds of sacrifice. Various notable events in U.S history ranging from the Great Depression, World War II, Brown vs. Board of Education to the Civil Rights Movement and the Million Man March of 1995 all demonstrate some display of substantial sacrifice.

These substantial sacrifices existed with one main goal; creating a better life for future generations. Those soldiers of sacrifice clearly understood that it wasn't about them. They used their voices, positions, talents, energy, resources, connections, strength, unity, creativity, passion and faith to ensure that the unborn would live in better conditions than what they were currently experiencing. As you look back on the three scriptures that began this point, they each speak true to communal sacrifice.

John 3:16 speaks to the ultimate sacrifice made by God and Jesus for the benefit of all humanity. God sacrificed his only begotten son for all believers.

Philippians 2:4 speaks to *Service for Society* in which we should always have our minds fixed not solely on what want we want, but what we can do to bless our fellow brothers and sisters. When we keep the needs of others in our hearts, this demonstrates part of God's plan for our lives.

Proverbs 27:2 speaks to the fact that the abundance of self-praise can be unhealthy. We are to let praise come from others and go to God in reference to our accomplishments. Speaking positive words to your spirit is encouraged. However, a hyper-saturation of self-praise will lead to arrogance, entitlement, and a disregard for the needs of others.

In short, be proud of yourself, but leave the praises about yourself to others. I encourage everyone reading these pages to manifest that concept within you. **To whom much is given, much is required**. This speaks to the notion that we all have an appointed individual responsibility to affect change and advancement for those other than ourselves.

Key XV: Walk in Victory!

Romans 8:37 I can do all things through Christ who strengthens me. In all these things we are more than conquerors through him who loved us.

2 Corinthians 9:8 And God is able to make all grace abound to you so that in all things at all times, having all that you need, you will abound in every good work.

Failure is NOT an option. This truly needs no further explanation. A *Walk in Victory* is essential to achieving full development and success. You must call things that are not as if they already are. In the 2005-06 basketball season, an unknown team from a small university in the Virginia area made history in the NCAA basketball tournament. George Mason University turned the college basketball world on it ear when they advanced to the NCAA Final Four. Many NCAA basketball fans had not even heard of GMU, let alone thought they would advance to the big dance. GMU was a low seed that barely made it in the tournament, and they were viewed just like other no name schools in basketball.

On their way to the NCAA Final Four, they defeated some of the most impressive squads in college basketball that year. Soon there were suddenly George Mason University fans nationwide. People began to take notice and eventually ask the question, "Who is George Mason University and how are they defeating such talented teams?" They gave the Cinderella-team reference new meaning. School paraphernalia such as t-shirts jerseys and the like sold out campus-wide within days. Their David and Goliath-like performance throughout the tournament demonstrated how this small school with a big heart actually **Walked In Victory**.

How did they do it? They carried themselves as if they belonged in that tournament. Throughout interviews with numerous George Mason players, the comment was consistent among the entire team. "We don't want to play like we're just glad to be here, we want to play like we actually belong." Although they didn't win the championship, the heart, determination, and champion-like character that they displayed will put them down as one of the most heroic and tenacious teams in NCAA tournament history. George Mason University's Basketball Team Walked in Victory.

This statement speaks volumes to each of us. When we are striving for excellence, we are to carry ourselves like we belong where we desire to be, not where we currently are. Whether you are studying to win the local spelling bee or studying to win a big court case, you must carry yourself like you belong at your destination. If you want to be prosperous, you must think, behave, and carry yourself prosperously even though you may not have but a dime in your pocket. If you are not the smartest student in school, presenting yourself as studious is the very start you need to get to that goal.

There was once a mailroom clerk name Ted who came to work in a suit and tie. Each day he reported to work dressed in a suit and tie, (sometimes the same suit) just to perform his duties in the mailroom. His supervisors were shocked while his coworkers frequently mocked him. They continually and laughingly asked him "Why do you waste your time wearing suits to work in the mailroom?" His response was, **"I'm not dressing for the job I have, I'm dressing for the job I want, supervisor."** All the laughing ceased. Needless to say, Ted surpassed all of his mailroom colleagues in securing that supervisor's position in the company. Ted *Walked in Victory.*

Similar to mailroom clerk, now supervisor, Ted, and George Mason University's Basketball team, it is our obligation to think and behave in a victorious manner.
We are to accept that we are especially blessed with individual talents that will prove prosperous while actually sowing seeds in the lives of others.

We have not because we think not. What we must understand is two of the biggest barriers to our true potential and success is that what we think and what we speak affects how we walk, where, and how far we walk. When we begin to think in victory, and speak in victory, only then can we *"Walk In Victory."*

Are You Ready for a Better Way to Live Your Life?

From Mind to Movement

NO MORE READING; NO MORE FORGETTING. Here is your opportunity to actually write down your decisions and plan of action. The following are exercises that will enable you to visualize your thoughts. As stated earlier, you will be asked particular questions that will address applying these principles to your life. You don't necessarily have to fill in the allotted spaces immediately. Feel free to analyze for as long as you need, then come back and begin writing. Use extra paper if needed. I ask that even if you are not sure what your decision or plan of action is, use the space provided to list what you have learned about that particular key. This may assist you in determining your action at a later time.

Movement I: Don't Be Afraid to Be Different

Seriously think of what exactly will you do that is original, innovative cutting edge or in short, something that very few others around you are doing. What new ideas will you entertain? What new places and activities will you seek out? What will you represent that is unlike anything or anyone else around you? List in the space below the steps you will take to de different.

_____

_____

_____

_____

_____

_____

_____

_____

_____

_____

_____

_____

_____

Movement II: Surround Yourself with Positive People

You may find that you may have to add new people to your
circle and at the same time remove old ones. Think about
those who truly contribute positively, and those who make
substantial withdrawals. Can you live with or without those
individuals? What can you do to be a positive person in the
lives of others? Discuss your plan to ensure that you have as
many positive people around you as possible.

_____

_____

_____

_____

_____

_____

_____

_____

_____

_____

_____

_____

Movement III: Develop Your Mission Statement

Critically analyze what your mission statement will be. What are some major things you would like to address in your mission statement? Who do you wish to serve within your mission statement? In addition, contemplate your gift and what it will be to those you serve. Write below your mission statement, your focused gift, and how you will distribute your gift thus, executing your mission statement.

_____

_____

_____

_____

_____

_____

_____

_____

_____

_____

_____

_____

Movement IV: Keep God in Your Life

At this point I would like for you to think about your spiritual relationship with God. What can you do to enhance or improve that relationship? Think of the many things that you are grateful for and how your faith has contributed to these things. In the space below discuss steps you can take to have a stronger spiritual relationship (not traditional practices of religion).

_____

_____

_____

_____

_____

_____

_____

_____

_____

_____

Movement V: Never Compare Yourself to Others

Take this time to determine if you've made the mistake of
cross comparisons in the past. Have you compared your life
to that of friends, family, and coworkers only to feel slighted,
disappointed or ashamed? Explain what tactics you will use to
avoid unrealistic expectations due to comparisons to the lives
of others.

_____

_____

_____

_____

_____

_____

_____

_____

_____

_____

_____

_____

_____

Movement VI: Listen To Elders. There is Wealth in Their Wisdom

Each of us can think of someone who at one time planted a seed of wisdom in us. Think of individuals who you feel have wisdom to share that can affect your life. Explain your method of connecting with those individuals to obtain some life's lessons that could be quite beneficial to you.

_____

_____

_____

_____

_____

_____

_____

_____

_____

Movement VII: Re-Channel Your Energy/Redirect Your Focus

In this section we have discussed various examples of re-channeling our energy and redirecting out focus. You would be incredibly surprised to see the new things that you can do well if your "majority-energy" is applied.

Think of some of the ways that you spend your time or what dominates your energy and focus. Is there something you would like to see or do differently? If so, list examples of how you can reapply your thoughts and energy towards things that can yield a successful result in your life.

_____

_____

_____

_____

_____

_____

_____

_____

_____

Movement VIII: Sow a Seed

Sowing and reaping is a basic law of natural and spiritual harvest. If you understand this law, you'll clearly see that one of the best ways to get something is to GIVE something. How will you sow a seed? How will you give to your need? What seed will you sow?

Each of us has something unique to give. Please remember sowing a seed extends far beyond donating money. Specific talents, volunteered time, available resources, experiences, wisdom, connections, are just few things that can be sown that can enhance the lives of others. List below ways you will sow a seed into the lives of others.

Movement IX: Commit Your Life to Knowledge

As stated previously, education is not only for consumption but it is to be used to create new knowledge. If we all consumed the knowledge of this world without adding to that knowledge we would experience an arrested development. In what way will you expand your knowledge base? What will you seek to learn that you previously did not know? How can this new knowledge be used to help you achieve success?

Movement X: Plan "B" Is Not Recommended, It's Required

To guide you in writing your plan of action or basic thoughts about "Plan B"; I reintroduce the following questions:

1. Have I established what my "Plan B" actually is?
2. If I can't do my number one choice of occupation what else will I do?
3. Have I acquired the knowledge and talents necessary that will keep me successful in the event that my first choice doesn't work?
4. What are other things that I enjoy and I am good at that could result in a fulfilling and successful career?

_____

_____

_____

_____

_____

_____

_____

_____

Movement XI: Do Not Fear Challenge and Change

We now understand that change and challenge must be embraced and not feared. Key #11 has taught us that we must make an exodus from our comfort zone that makes us reliant on the normal way of things, which creates the notion to fear anything that resembles newness. One of the ways to prepare for change is to embark on new activities and new interests. Think of ways you will emancipate yourself from the fear of change. Think of ways to prepare for and better deal with challenges.

_____
_____
_____
_____
_____
_____
_____
_____
_____
_____
_____

Movement XII: Watch Your Mouth

We now know the power of our words. We know the potential consequences of phrases like "you're killing me," "you make me sick," or "I'm so broke I can't pay attention." We recognize that we speak our destiny. Think of things that you can begin to manifest in your life by speaking them outright. What new phrases of success, happiness, health, wealth, peace and joy will you add to your choice of words?

_____
_____
_____
_____
_____
_____

114

Movement XIII: "Cool and Cute" Won't Cut It

Reflect back and think of the times anyone you know has used being cute or cool as a way to achieve a certain result. How far did it get them? What ways have you seen being cute or cool result in negative consequences? What ways can you eliminate the desire to use superficial qualities to receive meaningful additions to your life. What attributes will you develop that will sustain any test of cute or cool?

_____

_____

_____

_____

_____

_____

_____

_____

Movement IVX: It's Not About You!

Ponder closely on the four words no one wants to hear but everyone needs to hear. Think of ways to re-channel your energy and talents in order to help another person, cause or effort. What can you do to improve your existence in life to be one that is not self-serving but is serving to others?

_____

_____

_____

_____

_____

_____

_____

_____

_____

_____

_____

Movement XV: Walk in Victory!

You are now ready. You are continuing to learn, grow, give
and serve. What new attitude will you adapt to ensure you no
longer live a life of defeat? What actions will you take that
will enhance your confidence in knowing that no matter what
the circumstance, you can overcome? What will others
observe differently about you now that you understand what
this Walk in Victory truly is?

_____

_____

_____

_____

_____

_____

_____

_____

_____

_____

THE TREE of CULTURAL TRADITION

The Transfer of Cultural and Generational Tradition.

When speaking on seeking a successful and fulfilling life, I refer to the model of the Tree of Cultural and Generational Tradition. The simple explanation of this model is that everything is connected and every part of a living thing is dependent on another.

In the instance of the tree, there are three major components which all have a vital function in the survival and life quality of the tree. The reference of the survival and quality of the tree is synonymous to the survival and quality of humankind. In this discussion, I will attempt to demonstrate how the components of a tree are exactly the same components needed for individuals, families, communities, and nations to acquire the generational abundance that comes with a victorious life. The three major components of the tree are as follows:

The Roots

The roots are the unseen yet most important part of the tree. The roots represent the foundation of life. Every living thing that grows from the earth has roots. The roots of the tree represent the system of circulation throughout the tree. The roots gain nutrients from the earth and circulate those precious minerals throughout the body of the tree. Now I know as you read this you say to yourself that you are well aware of the functions of a tree's Roots. However, I'm taking this explanation further.

The roots represent the past and the history. In terms of cultural and generational advancement, the roots represent the ancestors and elders of our community. In a figurative reference the roots lie underground representing the elders and ancestors of our community whose bodies lay below the earth's surface. The memories and lessons of their sacrifices are the nutrients of our cultural and generational tree. The roots represent the sacrifices made by those before us who made contributions sacrificially so that generations to follow could lead more prosperous and fulfilling lives.

Figurative roots of our cultural and generational include individuals such as Jesus, Moses, the generations of African slaves, Madam CJ Walker, George Washington Carver, Martin Luther King, Gandhi, WEB Dubois, Sojourner Truth, Malcolm X, Shirley Chisholm, Mahaila Jackson, Steven Biko, Medgar Evers, Nelson Mandela, the late NASA astronaut

Ronald E. McNair, Thurgood Marshall, Harold Washington, Countee Cullen, Paul Robeson, Charles Drew, Wilma Rudolph, and Betty Shabazz to name more than a few.

The aforementioned list may sound like a middle school Black History Month lesson naming historic notables in African American Society. However, this list includes but is not limited to our great grandparents, grand parents, (elderly or deceased) parents, aunts, and uncles. All of these individuals are considered roots in African American cultural and generational traditional tree. They are individuals who made some sacrifice in their lives in order for future generations to prosper.

The Trunk

The trunk is the most visibly solid part of the tree. The trunk of the tree is hard, firm and rough. This representation speaks to the current strength of the tree. The trunk is the protector of the tree that endures the current powerful storms, bitter artic winters and blazing heat indexes of summer.

The trunk represents our present. The figurative reference to the trunk is today's major contributors to the social structures of this world. The adults who work hard daily to create a better society are included in the trunk. These individuals may included Oprah Winfrey, Spike Lee, Earl Graves, Barack Obama, Kwesi Mfume, Tom Joyner, Jessie Jackson, Kirk Franklin, Ministers Louis Farrakhan, Miles Munroe, TD Jakes, Eddie Long, Dr. Bill Winston, NASA astronaut Mae Jemison, professors Henry Louis Gates, Lani Gaunier and Cornell West to name more than a few.

Similar to the reference list of the roots, the same applies for the trunk. This list includes everyday people who wonderful and blessed efforts go unnoticed to the newspaper staffs. These are the current day heroes of society who work hard for more than just a paycheck. Individuals to add to the trunk list include city and state officials, social workers, police officers, lawyers, doctors, nurses, professors, clergy members, teachers, counselors business owners, little league football coaches, postal carriers, musicians, bus drivers, architects, songwriters and authors. All of these individuals are considered trunks in African American cultural and generational traditional tree.

Branches and Leaves

Arguably the most noticeable yet weakest part of the tree, the branches and leaves demonstrate the future of the life of the tree. The branches extend far and long representing promise, potential and hope while green leaves show fertility, then change colors in fall representing growth and maturity. As you can probably guess the branches and leaves represent our future. Thus the individuals who represent the branches and leaves are our youth.

The children of our communities represent the promise and hope of our generation. This list includes the young students, volunteers, musicians, scientists, athletes, or basically any child with a dream. In terms of care for a tree the most attention is placed on the leaves and branches. Their particular appearance speaks to the overall health of a tree.

Therefore, if we want to assure the overall health and wealth of our future, we must invest in the lives of our youth, which are the branches and leaves of our generation. If our children are raised in a compromised state, then we run the likely risk of our future being just that, compromised.

The Transference of Tradition and Culture

The connection between the dynamics of tree growth and the development of generations is very self-explanatory.
The roots of the tree are substantially responsible for the overall growth of the tree. The nutrients from the earth that are gathered from the roots are transferred up through the entire structure of the tree, through the trunk and extending out to the leaves and branches. Thus, the health of the branches and leaves are directly affected by the health and effectiveness of roots. The elders speak to this in their statement, "***You can tell the root by its fruit.***"

The exact same thing happens in the growth of the cultural and generational tree. The actions taken, decisions made, and legacies left by the elders, affects the bloom of the future generation. Decisions, actions, philosophies, beliefs, customs, values, and traditions held by your grandparents have (in some way) affected particular aspects of your life and the lives of your children. This is the display of the transference of culture and tradition.

Another example would be to look at the presence of the educational and intellectual pioneers such as WEB Dubois, Carter G. Woodson and Mary McCloud Bethune. The impact of their challenges and successes paved the pathway for today's scholars such as Dr. Henry Louis Gates Jr., Dr. Jawanza Kunjufu, Dr. Johnetta Cole and Dr. Cornell West.

In addition, those elders of the intellectual movement are responsible for the very existence of many of America's Historically Black colleges and universities also known as

HBCU's such as Tuskegee University, Fisk University, and Bethune Cookman College.

In terms of entertainment, the seeds planted by individuals such as Sammy Davis Jr., Lean Horne, Dorothy Dandridge, the Nicolas brothers, Sarah Vaughn and Duke Ellington have blossomed in future seasons in the likes of: Michael Jackson, Marvin Gaye, Branford Marsalis, Mary J. Blige, Alicia Keys and Beyoncé. Once again, this is the display of the transference of culture and tradition.

What seeds will be planted?

The leaves on a tree in winter months fall to the ground to become part of the soil. As leaves break down, they assist in the fertilization of the soil. They serve as seeds. What will happen in the future depends on the types of seeds that are planted. If bad seeds are planted, the result will be weeds, crabgrass, or just barren dirt.

On the contrary, if good seeds are planted, one will see healthy grass and flowers. Now this is no lesson in horticulture, but a figurative reference to planting the proper seeds. When a community plants seeds of fear, ignorance, lack, mis-education, laziness, crime, hatred, drug abuse, poverty, dishonor, and envy, there are consequential blooms in future season. The results of planting those seeds are crime, teen pregnancy, violence, disrespect, increased school dropout rates, unemployment, imprisonment, low self-esteem, community distrust, child abuse, addiction and indifference.

This is usually illustrated in my speeches by using a diagram of a tree showing two sides of the tree. Once again, the types of seeds that are planted will determine whether you have weeds or grass, or whether you have a toxic or a healthy tree that grows bountifully. Thus, when discussing the cultural and generational tree, our duty is to make absolutely sure the healthy seeds far out number the toxic seeds. The type with the greatest numbers planted or the most potent seed strength will dictate the harvest.

Please understand that everything we do, from how our children are raised to how our communities are developed, counts as seeds planted which will bring forth a harvest of hope and healing or of toxins and despair.

Stop Listening So You Can Hear Me

Route 3:
Stop Listening So You Can Hear Me

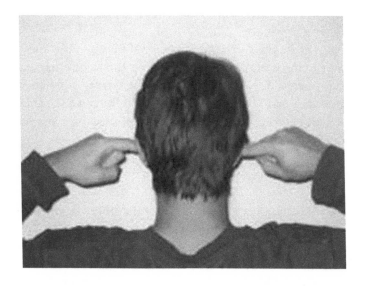

The Explanation

It Just Ain't, Still

The main message behind this piece is to inform the reader that not everything we see is as it appears. Your grandmother's voice rings truth as she says "Not everything that glitters is gold." We are witnessing a media based force feeding of someone else's fantasy commanding us to claim it as our reality. Not everyone who appears to be your enemy may necessarily be. At the same time, the greatest betrayal can come from your closest friend or most beloved family member.

We must take the responsibility to read between the lines of what is being written and hear between the words that are being spoken. We need to question the quality of what surrounds us and our families. Not everything we see and experience is true, pure, healthy, kind, precise, or real; thus, *it just ain't.*

No MTV Rotation

No MTV Rotation speaks to the fact that there is a mission to demonstrate expose or display a particular negative characteristic about things and people. This piece speaks to the constant barrage of negative toxic imagery and stories about a certain population, community or situation. Unfortunately, much of what is good in our society gets very little media exposure. School graduations don't get nearly the exposure that school murders do. Why are we more likely to hear about who was punished than who was promoted? The media mantra is, "If it doesn't bleed, then it doesn't read." We are inundated with more problems than actual solutions.

No MTV Rotation charges us to continue our blessed works even though the media may not be interested, our good works are appreciated. I implore the reader to take notice of this situation, but do not accept it. Do your great works not for the camera, but for the commitment.

Heart Failure

This was one of the most difficult and painful pieces to write. Heart Failure speaks to the figurative failing heart of our society's men. Hear Failure demonstrates how in some way the men of our community have dropped the ball of family protection and development. The man's neglect has left his family in a compromised and vulnerable state. The woman is angry, frustrated, and bitter. The daughters are lost in a quest for true love from a man. Consequently, they sacrifice themselves through dangerous sexual practices leading to molestation, teen pregnancy, disease, and domestic abuse. The sons are left to become men quickly with little to no instruction; thus, they exude manhood through anger, aggression, violence, confrontation and lack of respect for authority. Such attributes may lead him to a destiny of death or the death sentence. Heart failure is the poetic alarm clock to our men.

MLK Today Modern Day Nightmare

MLK Today simply asks the question, what would Dr. King think of the current state of African Americans if he were alive today? This poem was somewhat a monologue impersonating a modern day Dr. King on his frustration with the condition of our society. In this poem/monologue, Dr. King speaks in anger as to how in some ways the civil rights efforts have gone ignored and been disregarded. The quest for freedom and equality has now been replaced with a desire for status via consumption of meaningless and temporary things such as cars, clothes, and jewelry. Interestingly enough, cartoonist Aaron McGruder also did an episode of his animated television show *The Boondocks* on this very issue.

The World or the Word

This is more of a spiritual piece that is a reflection on the battle within us to either listen to the wisdom of man or heed the word of God. The inspiration derives from a quest for the ability to decipher between the two. Worldly theories and belief systems are compared with what the Bible says about particular situations. As believers of God, we are challenged daily to determine which will hold the most weight in our lives—the evidence of the world or the promise and faith of the word.

THEM

When it comes to difficulty in relationships, the question is always who is to blame for the chaos? Women say that it's men, and men say that it's women. I believe there are three sides to this issue—his, hers, and the truth. *THEM* was written as a warning to all of us about standing in our own way, blocking our blessings, and postponing our progress when it comes to loving relationships.

I attempt to speak candidly about our exposed shortcomings that include: misguided priorities, fear, greed, insecurity, unrealistic expectations, perfectionist pride, dependency on conflict/drama, and heeding relationship advice from unqualified and "disqualified" individuals. My attempt with THEM is to explain to the reader that if we simply get out of our own way and just live to love, success in relationships is possible.

Hip Hop Holocaust (Triple H)

As a child of the 80's, I was raised on hip hop in it's hey day. What my generation is witnessing now is a total overhaul of the art form. The duties of pre-millennium hip hop were to facilitate expression, heal the people from a societal ill, or to educate listeners to that societal ill. Triple H (as I call it) speaks to the frustrations of older hip hop fans based on the paradigm shift in the power of the music. I don't mean to go Cosby at this point, but there appears to be a toxic spirit within the music these days. The saturation of our community's ills delivered via BET and other media vehicles has given the music form a new face. Is that face healthy for our young listeners? Is it the political voice for urban youth that it once was? Or is it just an anthem for partying, consumption, self destruction, degradation of women, and senseless violence? The national debate continues.

In closing it is my hope that you have been entertained enlightened, educated and inspired. I hope this book will be used to help someone not only enhance their lives, but enhance the lives of others. It is my hope that you can take something from this text that will facilitate your **Walk in Victory**.

Your breakthrough is coming, and your blessing is here! God Bless.

Allen J. Bryson

Notes

References

Holy Bible: New International Version King James

Reverend Harold G. Blair, *Deep Thought Ministries*

Mr. LeRoy Brown Jr., *Fresh Manna for Today Ministries*

Bill Crowder, Dennis J. DeHaan, David C. Enger, *Radio Broadcast Ministries*

Dennis Fisher, Haddon W. Robinson, David Roper, *Our Daily Bread. Bible Gateway Ministries*

Dr. William Winston, Living Word Christian Center

Recommended Reading

Its Not Over Until You Win: How to Become the Person You Always Wanted to Be No Matter What the Obstacle by Les Brown

Live Your Dreams by Les Brown

Reposition Yourself: Living Life Without Limits by T.D. Jakes

Your Best Life Now: 7 Steps to Living at Your Full Potential by Joel Osteen

Winning 101: Devotional by Van Crouch

Think and Grow Rich! The Original Version
by Napoleon Hill

*Dare to Succeed: A Treasury of Inspiration and Wisdom for Life and
Career* by Van Crouch

*Who Moved My Cheese? An Amazing Way to Deal with Change in
Your Work and in Your Life*
by Spencer Johnson and Kenneth Blanchard

The Cornel West Reader
by Cornel West

Life Strategies: Doing What Works, Doing What Matters
by Phillip C. McGraw

Tours and Seminars

For information on Allen J. Bryson's tours and seminars, visit:

Website: www.ajbryson.com

Feel free to contact author for speaking engagements, seminars, conferences, literary events, workshops, cultural shows, poetry performances, appearances and consulting.

E-Mail: ajbryson@sbcglobal.net

Allen J. Bryson

A native of Chicago Illinois, Allen J. Bryson is an author, poet, spoken-word artist, motivational speaker, and educational specialist. He has been writing and performing spoken-word and delivering speeches for ten years. He has shared the stage with speakers such as Harry Belafonte, Les Brown, and Minister Louis Farrakhan. He has opened up for celebrities such as BET's Bruce-Bruce, cultural icons THE

LAST POETS and performed at numerous conferences, concerts, and cultural shows. His university speaking appearances span from the University of Chicago to the University of Florida.

In addition, he was featured on Operation Push's morning broadcast with the Reverend Jessie L. Jackson Sr., which was seen in over 45 countries including over 10 million viewers in South Africa.

His first book **Sleeping With My Eyes Open…Deposit Slips of My Soul** has been applauded as one of the more powerful spoken word publications of today's new authors. He recently released his powerful performance and motivational speech DVD entitled, **There's a New Poet in Town.**

Bryson holds a Communications Bachelors and Educational Masters degree from the University of Illinois at Urbana–Champaign. He's a proud member of Alpha Phi Alpha Fraternity Inc. He has an impressive tenure of delivering motivational speeches and academic and cultural development seminars at churches, professional conferences, high schools, and universities throughout the country. He has been described as a Vessel of Victory, a Deacon of Deliverance, an Instrument of Inspiration, and an Agent of Advancement. His mission is to write, inspire, elevate, educate, and empower.

CPSIA information can be obtained
at www.ICGtesting.com
Printed in the USA
FSHW021437180419
57346FS

9 781598 250039